SENSATIONAL MEDITATION FOR CHILDREN

MINDFULNESS, GUIDED IMAGERY, AND OTHER CHILD-FRIENDLY MEDITATION TECHNIQUES

SARAH WOOD VALLELY

Satya Worldwide, Asheville, NC

Published by
Satya Worldwide.
Asheville, NC 28804
www.satyaworldwide.net

SECOND EDITION

Cover and Interior Design by Allison Deatherage
Cover Art by Sarah Wood Vallely
Illustration by Elizabeth Ward Schussler

Library of Congress Cataloging-in-Publication Data
Sarah Wood Vallely
Sensational Meditation: Mindfulness, Guided Imagery, and Other Child-Friendly
Meditation Techniques / by Sarah Wood Vallely
ISBN 0-979-3302-4-6
ISBN 978-0-9793302-4-7 (13 digit)
1. Mind/Body/Spirit 2. Meditation 3. Parenting
I. Title

For Jane Wood, my loving mother and cherished editor,
and for Royce Morales, my inspiration and my teacher.
Thank you both.

I would also like to thank Sarah Tower, Angela Marschall, and George
Chen for so generaously sharing their teaching stories with me,
which I have included in this edition.

CONTENTS

Introduction

A MEDITATION MOVEMENT FOR CHILDREN is quietly emerging across the United States and throughout the world. Children are learning meditation techniques at home, in school, in after-school clubs, and in churches, yoga studios, YMCAs, and other community centers. Parents, teachers, and therapists are finding that meditation helps children in as many ways as there are children learning its techniques.

Teachers who incorporate meditation techniques into their lesson plans report that their classroom environments are more peaceful. They attribute this to their students' ability to express care and compassion for one another. Teachers also say their students' academic skills and confidence have risen.

Therapists who work with children say meditation reduces test anxiety, builds positive peer relationships, and enhances anger management skills. Scientists find meditation decreases blood pressure and helps other physical functions, which may be adding to these positive shifts in children.

Parents are also beginning to grasp moments of serenity and bliss after teaching meditation techniques to their children. Parents say meditation helps their family members be more respectful of one another; thus relationships grow closer and more fulfilling. Some parents say meditation helps raise their children's self-esteem. Aditionlly, children now can relax in doctors' offices and wind down at bedtime. Their health has improved, too. Parents report that their children truly like to meditate, are curious about its processes, and ask lots of questions.

Many children say that meditation helps them prepare for tests and sports events; and report it improves their relationships with their friends, parents, brothers, and sisters. Other children tell me that they like to meditate because it helps them feel happier when they are sad, and sometimes simply because it's fun. One child shares, "It just feels cool!"

So how does meditation bring about these changes, these attitudes and feelings? Is it conscious breathing or focused attention on a single object? Is it connecting to an extraordinary dimension of being? Is it discipline, or is it letting go so children can face their biggest fears and their most fantastic dreams?

I offer two types of meditations in this book: mindfulness and journeying. Mindfulness meditation involves bringing our awareness into the present moment by noticing what we experience through our senses. Journeying allows us to navigate through our consciousness to bring forth healing (often referred to as *guided imagery*). This type of meditation introduces symbolism, which children do not necessarily need to interpret to experience its benefits.

Both of these techniques (mindfulness and journeying) offer children two important benefits. The first is a forum for practice. Children can practice any activity, such as concentrating on their breath, which helps them develop overall concentration. However, this is only one example of what children can practice during meditation. Other skills include math, anger management, social skills, and athletics.

The other important benefit children gain from both mindfulness and journeying meditation is self-awareness. Meditation helps children become more deeply aware of who they are. With meditation, children better understand their feelings, learn their needs, and realize their own potential.

Many of the exercises I offer are journey meditations. They are *semi-guided*: children are led through a story that they help create. These meditations are designed to bring children to a certain point, after which they use their imagination to form the rest of their experience. These journey meditations are not visualizations, but instead are experiences powered by what children hear, feel, and even taste and smell, in addition to what they see. I refer to this experience as *sensational meditation*. Sensational meditation is also achieved during mindfulness meditations. Children rely on their senses to help them become fully present.

I also highlight the imaginative properties of meditation and show how meditation can heal and bring clarity. The techniques shared in this book are borrowed from many different traditions, including ancient yogic, Polynesian, and Buddhist practices as well as from modern clinical therapy. Although this book delves into different traditional meditation practices, it constantly brings to light the important role the senses play in meditation. When we or our children meditate, our senses light up and explode in a sensory awakening that activates our inner channels, which leads to clarity and confidence. This, of course, helps children thrive socially, academically, and physically.

When I began offering meditation classes to children, many adults showed up to see how I could possibly persuade, influence, or inspire children to meditate. Parents observed; visitors without children watched and learned. But only some of the elements of my success can be understood by witnessing alone. I use a well-developed approach and philosophy that supports each move. I will share its secrets with you. I will show you how to facilitate learning through fun and through games. You will learn how each child is unique and that there is not one sure-fire approach that works for all.

The biggest secret I will share with you is the transformation that we adults experience when we become partners in learning with our children. Developing a meditation practice is a journey in growth, whether it is spiritual, emotional, or mental. When we partner with our children, we grow and excel with them. For me, this is the most exhilarating aspect of my work.

No matter how old your children are, you can become their partner in learning. If your child is at least five years old, he will benefit from most of the techniques in this book. (A few meditations are better suited for children eight years and older.) If your child is younger than five, I suggest you learn the techniques provided and model them. You can sit quietly with your eyes closed for a few minutes once or twice a week in front of your child. Your curious toddlers and preschoolers will ask what you are doing, and occasionally they might even join you. This is a perfect way to introduce meditation to this age group. Nevertheless, some children as young as three years old successfully use the meditations in this book. So if your child is younger than five, use your best judgment as to when the best time is to begin.

I welcome you as you embark on an extraordinary, exciting and fulfilling voyage with your child. Move through these pages as if you were reading a mystery. Discover my secrets for working with children—what *sensational* truly means—and discover all the ways meditation enhances your life and your children's lives.

Remember, meditation is an adventure just the blink of an eye away. It is for anyone, child or adult, who dares to journey into his incredible imagination and tranquil solitude. It creates space to laugh and giggle, sing, and shout for joy. No meditator needs a monastery or other heightened setting—a child can meditate in a classroom, on a swing, or in a tent made of couch cushions and blankets.

chapter 1

MEDITATION HELPS CHILDREN NURTURE MIND, BODY, AND SPIRIT

YOUR CHILD WILL GAIN MANY REWARDS from learning how to meditate. Meditation will help her focus, experience the mind/body connection, and rejuvenate her spirits. This simple practice gives your child tools to explore her inner world with all her senses. Undoubtedly, these skills will continue to benefit her into adulthood, through university studies, career, relationships, or personal growth experiences. The person who discovers new ground in her consciousness is an evolving person, a new woman each time she meditates.

CULTIVATING MINDS—CREATIVITY AND FOCUS

Increased Creativity: *Creative* minds excel in today's society. Innovation is everywhere and sprouts from those intellects that make room for imagination. As I write this book, I stop from time to time to rest my mind and let the concepts flow as they will. Sometimes I do this with my eyes open and other times with my eyes shut. During these breaks, I am in a meditative state that allows my creativity to manifest. When I continue to write again, my mind is filled with creative ways to convey my thoughts.

Children experience this same phenomenon when they meditate. This is apparent in the drawings they create after meditation. The artwork is alive with creative shapes and colors. Meditation offers the child's mind a chance to be creative, thus nurturing her budding intellect. Another example of meditation's effectiveness is when in meditation children re-experience concepts they have learned from others and make them their own. An eight-year-old student told me that during one meditation she saw herself riding a horse along the Potomac River with George Washington. The abstract idea from an earlier history lesson became personal, and therefore part of the reservoir of experiences upon which she can now draw.

Better Focus: Meditation not only opens our minds but also offers a perfect *forum* for focus and practice. In the *Tao Te Ching*, the ancient Chinese philosopher Lao Tzu wrote: "Only when the cup is empty is it at its most useful."[1] The quiet space we rest in during meditation gives us the opportunity to empty our minds. We can let the chatter and worries subside for a bit. Ironically, this letting go of focus provides us with a blank slate of infinite potential. It creates a stage upon which we can achieve our goals, because as a result of meditating we are open, patient, and focused throughout the day.

Research shows when we practice a process mentally, we can successfully repeat it in the real world. A study, conducted by the Cleveland Clinic Foundation, found that when we visualize flexing our muscles, in the end, we physically change our muscle strength. During this study, one group of participants mentally flexed their little finger abduction muscle for fifteen minutes a day over the course of twelve weeks. Another group, who served as the control, did not perform these mental exercises. Surprisingly, the group who mentally worked out increased their muscle strength by 30%, while the control group showed no change in strength.[2]

The point here is that when we practice something during meditation it makes a difference afterwards, whether we are developing physical muscle or cultivating healthier outlooks. When we meditate and practice processes, such as letting go of thoughts and feelings that fuel our anger, we truly become better at managing strong emotions. The Grounding Cord meditation in Chapter 8 is an excellent example of a meditation that helps us improve our ability to release feelings that make it difficult for us to function harmoniously.

Meditation is not just a function of wishful thinking or overcoming mental blocks. Mental acuity actually improves because of meditation. Studies have shown that meditation synchronizes the wave patterns in our right and left brain hemispheres. When these hemispheres are in sync, they communicate more effectively with one another, and therefore function with more clarity and focus. Next time you have a complicated task to achieve—filing, for example, or writing a report—meditate for five minutes before you tackle the task. Notice if the activity seems a bit easier than usual after you meditate. If this works for you, then you will have experienced how meditation can help your child become more focused when performing her most challenging tasks.

Meditation enables children to focus in school and actually helps raise test scores. Although I do not always find standardized test scores a reliable indication of performance, studies indicate that children who meditate can raise their test results. College students at Maharishi University of Management were taught Transcendental Meditation and practiced it for two years. IQ tests were given to students practicing meditation, as well as to a control group of students who were not. The IQ scores of the meditators steadily rose over two years, while the non-meditators' IQ scores remained the same. The meditators' ability to quickly make choices also increased.[3]

In another study, elementary and high school students practiced Transcendental Meditation for one year. Their math scores on standard state exams surged from beneath the fortieth percentile to greater than the sixtieth percentile, and in reading from about the sixtieth percentile to the seventy-fifth percentile. Their overall academic achievement also increased.[4]

REDUCING STRESS

Sarah Tower works at a non-medical cancer wellness center, supporting cancer patients and their families through all stages of cancer. Most of the young clients Sarah works with have siblings or parents struggling with cancer. For example, Tim's dad has cancer. His mom is sad, and both of his parents are at the doctor's much of the time. Tim and other children in similar circumstances greatly benefit from Sarah's children's relaxation group.

Sarah begins each class by asking, "What is going on this week that makes you feel stressed?" Children bring up anything from a bad test grade to disappointment about their mom's lab results. Next, Sarah turns on soothing music. She asks the children to sit on yoga mats with their hands on their bellies. The children take deep breaths, feeling their bellies expand under their hands. They imagine a pole going through their bodies, from the top of their heads down their spines. This helps them sit straight and raise their shoulders.

Sarah guides the children to notice how the music makes them feel.

After ten minutes of breathing, Sarah leads the children through a variety of yoga positions for twenty-five minutes. Their yoga session is concluded with a *sponge pose*—lying on their backs with palms facing up for ten minutes. This time also serves as a bathroom break for those who need it.

Next, Sarah leads the children through a guided meditation. I was amazed to learn that Sarah's students between the ages of five and twelve years old spend a complete hour and a half engaged in relaxation. In Chapter 5, I share some of her secrets for keeping her students engaged.

As a result of Sarah's classes these children, who face tremendous anxiety surrounding cancer, reduce their stress. The children are able to identify when they are stressed and take action to calm themselves down, whether it be to take deep relaxing breaths or to go into a quiet room and turn on calming music.

SUPPORTING BRAIN DEVELOPMENT AND HEALING TRAUMA

The younger the child, the faster her brain develops. Our brains are made up of impulse-carrying neurons. These neurons connect at synapses, which are essentially gaps between neurons. As we grow we create more and more synapses. Synapses that are used frequently are reinforced, while those used less frequently or not at all are lost. This process *wires up* our body, which plays a role in how we experience our world.

A three-year-old has billions more synapses than the average adult. Eventually, during childhood and adolescence, children lose a great number of these synapses. Because a child's environment has an enormous impact on this selection process[5], meditation might help children maintain synapses related to intuition, creativity and inner focus.

In addition to supporting brain development, meditation helps children heal from trauma. Belleruth Naparstek, psychotherapist and author of *Invisible Heroes: Survivors of Trauma and How They Heal*, writes that "trauma *lives* in the right side of our brains where images, body sensations and feelings are stored—so it is best to heal trauma with right brain activity—working with images, body sensations and feelings." She offers that meditation and visualizations are the best ways to heal from a traumatic event.

Naparstek goes even further to explain that if we use talk therapy exclusively to overcome a traumatic event or events, our symptoms can get worse instead of better. This is important to consider, since children are far more vulnerable to traumatic stress than adults are.

Many people who learn about the benefits that children gain from a simple meditation practice wonder why schools avoid teaching it. There is good news in this regard: meditation is slowly making its way into our education system. Schools in Connecticut, Georgia, Colorado, Michigan, California, and Ontario, Canada, are already incorporating it into classrooms and counseling sessions for various age groups. These schools include public, charter, magnet, and private.

Even more encouraging, some of these programs are funded by not-for-profit and corporate organizations such as the American Heart Association, the National Institute of Health, Chrysler, and General Motors. Funds from these sources enable schools to hire professional meditation instructors.

After careful follow-up study of these programs, the consensus is that meditation does have many important benefits for children. Teachers report students are more introspective; they have higher self-esteem, better focus, and improved reading skills. Teachers also say that the number of fights in their schools has decreased because students have better relationships with their classmates, talk about their feelings more, make fewer snap judgments, and are, overall, happier people.

In order to appreciate these positive results, you might ask what specific techniques were taught to these young meditators. Some of these programs teach Transcendental Meditation (TM), which involves repeating a word or phrase throughout the meditation. Although TM is an effective method, other methods used in schools include both breathing and journey meditation, during which the child imagines being in certain places and doing certain things. This book includes all of these methods.

The following example shows how a journey meditation helps a child cultivate her mind. For a full description of this meditation exercise, see Chapter 8.

Ten-year-old Rosa has had difficulty in math class since the new school year began three months ago. Her father elects to lead her through the "Grounding Cord" meditation, which helps remove obstacles. During her meditation, Rosa experiences a large, red, prickly ball moving out of her body and down her grounding cord. She feels a scratchy feeling as she watches it push its way down. After it falls, she sees a smiling princess come out of a hole that was previously blocked by the ball. Rosa's father asks her if she would like to practice a math problem in her meditation with the princess's help. Rosa imagines picking up a magic wand with magic ink and writes on the outside wall of her imaginary castle. Rosa and the princess successfully complete three math problems offered by her father before she comes out of the meditation.

Using a grounding cord in meditation helps children find calmness and focus. Such meditations are grounding because they balance us with the natural rhythms of the earth, resulting in physical stability and emotional ease. Rosa experiences energies moving down her grounding cord. When children release energies from their beings, they let go of things that weigh them down, such as worry, anger, and despair. These feelings are worthy of attention, of course, but sometimes children hold on to these feelings when they do not need to. When they let go, they can focus more energy and attention on other subjects and ideas.

HEALING PHYSICAL AILMENTS

The development of the mind/body connection is a well-known benefit of meditation practice. Studies show that meditation helps prevent or reduce cancer, respiratory disorders, digestion problems, heart disease, and immune disorders. Dr. Richard Davidson, Professor of Psychology and Psychiatry at the University of Wisconsin at Madison, published a study showing that meditation increases levels of immunity. Half of the participants in this study underwent an eight-week-long meditation training. Then all those participating in the study received a flu shot. One month after the shots were given, all the participants' antibody levels were checked. Those who received the meditation training showed a 43 percent increase in antibodies over the non-meditators.[6]

There are many reasons why working with our minds heals our bodies. Sitting still and relaxing our minds affects us physiologically: our cell chemistry, heart rate, and other body functions respond positively. Since the subconscious mind controls the body's functioning, hypnotherapists believe that we can affect bodily functions by communicating with our subconscious during states of deep consciousness like those achieved when hypnotized or meditating. Employing our inner senses of seeing, hearing, and feeling allows us to "talk" with our physical bodies via our subconscious. I will discuss this inner sensing in more detail in Chapter 2

Children easily communicate with their bodies. Sometimes they see symbolic images, hear words, or get a sense of what is happening in their bodies through what they see, hear, and feel. They trust their senses. Even before my daughter learned how to meditate, at two years old, she told me that her "foot was upset." This type of communication with our bodies is more natural than one might think.

Four-year-old Madison had suffered from asthma for at least a year. Since she began using the meditation techniques in this book, she has been medication free. Her mother says, "Prior to our meditation practice, we were treating her every month. Now she talks about feeling that her mind is powerful enough to tell her body what to do. Meditation is part of our morning routine."

I also use meditation to help me understand and heal my body. On one occasion, I "spoke" with my body, and gained the understanding that I needed to alleviate my symptoms of TMJ (temporomandibular joint syndrome) or locked jaw. After closing my eyes, I instantly felt drawn to noticing the following symbolism, which I observed with my inner sense of sight. I saw a vision of prisoners standing behind bars in a jail cell trying to escape. It then occurred to me, my jaw was locked because it was afraid these prisoners would escape. After more meditation, I realized the prisoners represented thoughts I wanted to express to others, but for some reason felt I couldn't. As a result, I made an effort to speak my mind more freely. Within a few days, my jaw unlocked and my TMJ was relieved.

Some meditators may not see visions such as these and instead simply feel better physically after they focus on their breath during meditation or employ other mindfulness techniques. In fact, these methods have been extremely helpful for me personally in relieving any reoccurring TMJ symptoms.

Hypnotherapy, other forms of metaphorical journeying, and mindfulness are not the only ways we can heal our physical bodies with meditation. Yoga is an ancient practice—over 5,000 years old—that originated in northern India and offers an eight-limbed path to unite body and spirit, and attain enlightenment. In some forms of yogic meditation, the meditator visualizes his seven chakras, which correspond to different areas in the body. Chapter 9 discusses this practice in more detail.

The following are two examples of children using meditation to heal their bodies.

~ **Seven-year-old Lauren's tummy hurts. In meditation, Lauren asks her tummy what it needs. She hears from within that her tummy needs a tummy rub and soup.**

~ **Five-year-old Alberto complains that his throat is sore. His mother guides him through the "Strengthening Your Chakras" meditation. During his meditation, Alberto visualizes warm, healing energy going into his throat.**

RENEWING SPIRIT

Sometimes I take a warm bath or eat healthy food when I want to renew my spirit, and other days I meditate, which offers the same kind of sensual renewal. In meditation, children and adults alike can shower themselves with soothing energy and feed themselves with supportive feelings, images, and sounds, and even fruitful smells and tastes. For example, while meditating I might visualize dolphins swimming around me, hear their calls, see their sweet faces, and feel the warm ocean water lap up against me. This renews me and lasts well beyond my meditation session. I feel this positive energy coursing through me as I go about my day. On a physical level, this meditation stimulates the areas in my brain that are responsible for triggering the chemicals that allow me to feel euphoric or have a heightened sense of well-being.

Dr. Charles Raison, professor of psychiatry at Emory University, conducted a study on the affects of meditation on college students' depression and stress. One participant, Eliot Johnson, shares, "I definitely felt happier. Just comparing finals that semester with the semester before, it was a lot less stressful."[7] Children enjoy being led through nurturing journey meditations, too. Lauren sees herself gliding across a lake on a magic, fluffy dragon. She imagines listening to fish jump in the water while she reaches down to run her hands through the dragon's soft fur. She giggles with excitement and is renewed. Nothing is out of the ordinary for a child who can access her imagination, and meditation can give her the same jolt of energy I carry with me as I rise from my meditation to go about my day. She too will feel positive energy coursing through her as she does her homework or plays with friends or helps out with chores.

The late Dr. Leo Buscaglia, well-known author, educator, and public speaker, challenged his students to answer this question: "Who is the new child we are educating, and what are his needs?" He went on to say, "It isn't enough to live and learn for today. We have to dream about what the world is going to be like in fifty years and educate for a hundred years hence and a dream world of a thousand years hence. The world today for the first grader is not going to be his world in thirty years."[8] Dr. Buscaglia wrote this in 1972, and he was right. If we can empower children to find their own sense of peace, they will move through future challenges more easily.

The following examples further illustrate the power of meditation to refresh children's spirits. For a full description of these meditations, see Chapter 10.

~ Leo feels anxious the night before his science test. His mother leads him through the "Fudge Swirl" meditation to help relieve his anxiety. During this meditation, Leo brings an energy ball filled with confidence into his body.

~ Five-year-old Angela is angry with her stepbrother Alex for injuring her favorite doll. Alex has left for his mother's house and won't be able to speak to her about it until next week. Angela's step-father leads her through the "Healing Heart" meditation, during which Angela feels a path of energy between her heart and her stepbrother's heart. Afterward, she says she feels better and doesn't mind waiting until next week to talk to Alex about her doll and her feelings.

WHAT IS YOUR PURPOSE?

I know that some of you reading this book are novices, just beginning on the path of meditation. Even if the first time you meditate is during one of the exercises in this book, you are on course to be successful in teaching your child how to meditate.

Whether you have been meditating for years or are a first time meditator, before teaching meditation to children, I ask you to declare your personal purpose for doing so. Consider the reasons why you meditate; then think about how your child might benefit.

When I work with children I know that I am *teaching meditation to children* not *teaching children to meditate.* That is, I show children meditation tools, but the choice is theirs whether to use them or not. Consider this subtle shift in perspective when you formulate your purpose.

EXERCISE 1

Why Do I Wish to Teach Meditation to My Child?

Write in your journal or notebook your reasons for teaching meditation to your child. Feel free to use any benefits I've covered, as well as advantages not mentioned, and anything you have learned from your own experience as a meditator, whether that is a little or a lot of experience. What is your personal philosophy regarding children and meditation?

Be with your response to this question for a few days, and make changes as you discover more about your reasons for teaching meditation to children. Your clarity will help you to show your child the power of meditation.

chapter 2

THE TEN SENSES AND THE
FULL SENSATIONAL EXPERIENCE

WE ARE SENSUAL BEINGS HAVING SENSATIONAL EXPERIENCES.
I wake up in the morning to the *sound* of my daughter's cry. I *feel* the
soft sheets brush against my legs. I open my eyes to *see* the morning
sun break through the slits of my bedroom shade. After scooping up
my daughter, I go into the kitchen and *taste* a tangy orange, while
enjoying the *smell* of the scrumptious meal my husband prepares for
us. I am alive.

Aristotle delineated the five senses we all understand today.
Buddhists, however, have long talked about the sixth sense (mind);
and scientists now speak about at least 13 senses, including equilib-
rium, temperature, and hunger.[1] We will initially examine the five
senses identified by Aristotle because they are the most commonly
recognized; but at this point it is important that you also value
any other sensations you experience which do not fall into these
five categories.

OUR FIVE SENSES

Smell, hearing, taste, sight, and touch—these senses let us know what
is happening in our environment. When I wake up in the morning
to my daughter's cry, the sunlight, and soft sheets, I experience the
world around me. My senses make it possible for me to perceive and
enjoy these outer events. The senses are in fact our interface with the
world outside.

Our five senses both uplift us and pull us down. They do more than simply give us factual data about our world; they have a profound affect on how we feel and think. They inspire emotions. Or my inner world inspires these outer events. Either way, I feel happy listening to children playing in the park. When I look at colorful blossoms and smell their flowery fragrance, I feel joyful, exhilarated, and nostalgic all at once. At the same time, an ache in my back reminds me to relax and can even be a pleasant reminder of my work in the garden earlier that day. Itchy eyes let me know it is time to call it a night.

In short, the senses form a complex and important mechanism that helps us perceive the world. They trigger reactions in us, whether present moment or remembered emotions.

Our senses not only relay information about our world, they also play an important role in our ability to find and inhabit the present moment, whether we are involved in a conversation, driving, or medi-tating. I like to refer to this state of mind as being mindful. When we practice this kind of meditation, we are trying our best not to drift off into thoughts about the past or future, only entertaining what is happening *right now*. Thoughts about our shopping list or the parking ticket we received yesterday bring us out of a mindful state (unless we spend the moment noticing this is indeed where our mind has gone to). At the same time that we are letting go of our memories and fantasies, we are trying to overcome thoughts about people and things in other places (not here). For example, notions of our child in the other room or the beautiful weather in another state take us away from our personal present moment .

To help ourselves stop thinking about other things and other places, we can listen to, touch, and even look at what is happening right here, right now. For this reason, some meditation practices require meditators to keep their eyes open during meditation—focused softly on the floor in front of them, for example. *Looking* occupies their vision so they become less distracted by mind-invented images of people, places, and things elsewhere.

Using our sense of *hearing* also helps us avoid thoughts that bring us out of a mindful state. Next time you meditate, listen. Is there a fan blowing? Is there a clock ticking? Focusing on sounds helps turn off the inner voice of past and future.

Our sense of *touch* helps us become more mindful Next time you meditate, feel your body resting on the floor or other surface on which you are sitting or lying down. Feel your heartbeat with your hand. Notice any pain or tightness in your body. Sometimes I am grateful for pain because it gives me something to focus on during meditation.

Taste and *smell* can also keep us present. During meditation, notice what you smell. Can you pick up a scent of essential oil on your wrist? Can you smell dinner cooking? Can you taste anything: bitter, sweet, sour? Although I do not use my senses of taste and smell as often as I use my other senses to become more mindful, sometimes I find them helpful.

As much as our senses ground us in the present moment, they also have the power to project us into the past and future, or even somewhere else! We will look at this more closely in Chapter 8, but for now consider that mindfulness meditation is a gentle process of finding focus, losing it, and then gently finding focus once again. This is a practice in mindfulness: we do not judge our loss of focus, but instead simply notice it.

Children easily use their five senses to practice focus and enjoy tranquility. Eight-year-old Nyah sometimes feels uneasy about her classmates and school assignments. Her school counselor taught her a meditation technique that helped Nyah find her own sense of inner peace during these moments. In meditation, Nyah feels her back pressing against her chair, listens to silence broken by the pitter-patter of feet in the hallway outside her counselor's office. Then she notices that the back of her eyelids look like the night sky, sparkling with stars. She breathes deeply to smell the citrus air-freshener that lingers in the office. She takes a juicy raspberry from her lunch bag and places it in her mouth, taking her time to taste the tang and the sweetness it offers. This meditation helps Nyah calm her nerves and prepare for her next challenge.

The *"Mindfulness,"* "Me and My Zen," and "Me and My Mantra" meditations and in Chapter 8 are all excellent meditations created specifically to help children find inner peace in moments of stress.

OUR FIVE ADDITIONAL INNER SENSES

Let's now go beyond Aristotle's basic categorization of five senses and look into the more complex dimensions of ourselves as sensational beings. After tasting, touching, smelling, hearing, and seeing, the next level of our being is less tangible. For example, I taste my aunt's blueberry pie and its delicate sweetness brings me joy, but what if I close my eyes and *imagine* having a bite of my aunt's pie instead? Do I taste it? Do I feel joy from its deliciousness? What if I heard a drum roll in my mind before I stood up to speak at a business meeting? What if I closed my eyes and saw bright light swirling around me? Would I be having a sensational experience even though these events do not occur in my outer world?

I would say, yes. Not only do we physically experience smells, sounds, tastes, images, and feelings, but we also have these experiences in meditation and during other inward activities when we use our *inner senses.* Before I awaken to the cry of my daughter and the sunlight in the window, I am dreaming. I *see* red mountains and *feel* the rocky earth beneath my feet. I *hear* the hooves of a hundred horses. Once I had a lucid dream (I knew I was dreaming) in which the scientist in me took advantage of this conscious experience. In the dream I touched a table and felt the smooth surface of the wood. I touched the wall and felt the little bumps left by the paintbrush. I thought to myself, "I'm dreaming, yet I can feel these surfaces as if they are purely real." Although dreaming is different than meditating, the awareness of inner senses during these states of consciousness is similar.

When I talk to children in meditation class about their ability to see pictures in their minds and hear an inner voice, they usually offer imagination as the explanation. Imagination refers to the perception of images, sounds, smells, textures, and tastes when there is no stimulation of the sense receptors from the outer world. By definition, these children are correct. When, during meditation or while we are engaged in other inwardly-focused activities, we experience smells, sounds, tastes, images, and feelings not picked up by Aristotle's five senses—we are imagining them. Young children have robust imaginations, but by the time we become adults most of us have forgotten how to experience inner worlds with our inner senses. In fact, according to William Tedford of Oberlin College, at around age six, children begin to lose this ability to imagine, replacing it with abstract reasoning.[2] But (and this is great news), this loss of imaginative ability is not necessary or inevitable, nor is it irreversible.

Although I use the word *imagination* to explain our five inner senses, I do not mean to belittle a child's meditation experience by saying, "Oh that's just her imagination." Imagination is the portal to higher realms of consciousness. Imagination is bigger and more important than most adults realize. Saying to a child, "It's just your imagination" is like telling Albert Einstein, "Oh, stop wasting your time thinking about light traveling through space: that's just your imagination." Imagination not only opens up worlds denied by most adults, but it also enables us to be creative in our daily lives.

I like to think that we have ten senses: five senses that allow us to perceive and experience the outer world and five additional senses that allow us to perceive and experience the inner (or nonphysical) world. No single sense or set of senses is more important than another. While our outer senses help us thrive in our physical world, our inner senses are equally important for growth and adjustment. They help us heal our mental, emotional, and spiritual selves because they are a bridge to these parts of ourselves.

The inner senses play an important role during journey meditations, in which we travel in our minds to wondrous places that seem far away, but in fact are part of us. They are a reflection of our inner being. We might be led by someone or we may lead our own experience. We might imagine we are on a beach: we imagine *feeling* the warm sun on our skin and the *sound* of waves, while we *visualize* seagulls gliding by. This imaginative experience helps us tap into the gentle, soothing part of ourselves that sometimes gets lost among the chaos and drama of life. During another journey, we might focus on a body pain, which leads us to hear and visualize a drum being played—a subconscious expression of the throbbing pain. Then we might summon an imaginary violin to play, soothing the pounding drum of our pain. These experiences are possible because of our ability to invoke our inner senses of sight, hearing, and touch.

Children love to use their inner senses during journey meditation. When I lead 12-year-old Nathan through the "Time Machine" meditation, he is thrilled to see the buttons and dials inside his spaceship-like time machine. Then he feels the machine start up with a jolt, followed by a steady vibration. When he arrives at his destination, he gets out of the machine to feel the gritty ground beneath his feet. He hears the zoom of a plane overhead and sees a cityscape filled with shiny colorful buildings. Nathan engages his five inner senses to help him fully experience this inner world. The journey meditation is, hands down, my students' favorite, and it gives them skills they need to enjoy other journey meditations that help them overcome challenges and heal emotionally.

Ten journey meditations are offered in Chapters 8 through 11. Some of my favorites are "What Does My Body Have to Say," "The Happy Tree," and "Time Machine." In these chapters, I discuss in more detail how children can use their five senses to bring their journeys to life.

FULL SENSATIONAL EXPERIENCE

We've discussed how we use our five *outer* senses and our five *inner* senses during meditation. Now, let us bring all ten senses together to enjoy a grand finale: what I call the *full sensational experience.*

Actually, this dramatic ending is far from exceptional. We experience our everyday life with all ten senses. We walk down the street and *see* the sun casting shadows on the ground, we *hear* the sound of a truck passing by, we *feel* a hunger pang in our stomach (outer senses). Similarly, we *feel* a twinge of excitement inside: somewhere that we can't quite pinpoint (inner sense). We might also remember the way our child *smells*, *hear* our inner voice sing our favorite melody, and then imagine how our dinner will *taste* (more inner senses). We are having a *full sensational experience.*

I imagine Einstein had a full sensational experience when he formulated his Theory of Relativity. He might have *envisioned* (inner) the sun and its weight in space as a billiard ball resting on a sheet. While he *looked* (outer) down at his notes, he might have *remembered* (inner) a past conversation with his good friend, the mathematician Marcel Grossmann, about mathematics and gravity. He might have *felt* (outer) tightness in his gut as he waited for an eclipse to take place, which would prove his theory right or wrong.

If we experience life with all ten senses, why not meditate using all ten senses as well? Sometimes I meditate sitting on my porch. I *listen* to crickets peep in the yard. I *visualize* a ball of light above my head. My ball of light grows and I *feel* a warm energy fill my body. I *smell* the autumn air, while I *hear* myself silently repeat a mantra. I *feel* the breeze brush against my face, and I am at peace. One of the best meditations we can practice is to simply *be* and notice our ten senses soaking up our physical and nonphysical worlds.

Children can notice what comes through their ten sensory channels during meditation, as well. Five-year-old Jess's father helps Jess fall asleep by leading her through the "Sleeping Cloud" meditation. Jess uses her *outer* senses to feel the muscles in her legs and arms relax. She also notices how itchy her tired eyes feel. She exercises her *inner* senses by picturing a soft puffy purple cloud floating above her. She listens peacefully to her imaginary cloud playing her favorite lullaby, which helps her relax even more. Jess's senses help her drift into comfortable sleep.

All of the meditations provided in Chapters 8 through 11 are potentially full sensational experiences. The "Sleepy Cloud" in Chapter 8, however, specifically offers guidance to engage both your child's outer and inner senses.

This next exercise will help you open up to your ten senses, which in turn will help you guide your child to become comfortable using her inner senses.

EXERCISE 2

A Full Sensational Experience

Wherever you are, whatever you're doing, stop. Breathe deeply and close your eyes. When your eyes are closed, your senses of hearing, touch, smell, and taste intensify. Listen to your outer environment. Take a deep breath. Do you smell any scents in the air? Feel your hands. Are they smooth or rough? Are you tasting something right now? Turn your attention inside and focus on your inner being. Are you experiencing any emotions? If not, play with an emotion. *Pretend* you are feeling that emotion. Can you hear anything that is not in your outer world: maybe a song or someone's voice? Take your time. See your favorite pie under your nose. Can you smell it? Take a bite of your imaginary pie. Can you taste it? Now, imagine nothing in particular. Watch what happens. Be an observer of your own experience. Notice what you see, hear, feel (including emotions), taste, and smell in your outer and inner environment.

You might notice that some parts of this exercise were easier for you to do than others. Even becoming aware of one or two inner senses in a single meditation is beneficial; most adults have suppressed their inner senses for so long that they need time and practice. Chances are, however, that if you invited a child to explore this exercise with you and then had her tell you about her meditative experience, you would be shocked at how vivid and acute her sensational experience was compared with your own. This is one of those instances in which you can learn much from listening to the young person you are leading on the meditation path. With practice, all ten of your senses will be on call, ready and willing to sense and relate your surroundings and inner universe—just as powerfully as the child's.

A MIRROR IS AS CLEAR AS IT IS POLISHED

Before I became a meditation teacher, I worked as an art teacher in both elementary and high school. I explained to my students that creating representational art is not so much about moving the medium across the paper to draw or paint as it is about our ability to see what we are depicting—to see both its contour and the negative space between and around the object. I encouraged students to stop drawing or painting for a moment and *look*. I asked them to visually experience the still life as fully as possible. By the same token, possibly the most liberating meditation we can do is to *stop and listen* or *stop and feel*.

Some people who believe they cannot meditate are simply trying to perceive something in meditation with a sensory channel that is difficult for them to use. It may have grown weak out of disuse. I had an adult meditation student a few years ago, Charlie, who said he had tried unsuccessfully to meditate for years. During class I led him through a meditation in which he was encouraged to feel what he was experiencing, in addition to seeing and hearing it. Afterward, Charlie was deeply moved. He told the class he had felt warmth in his chest when he was guided to move energy from the top of his head down to his tailbone. He said he'd felt tingling in other areas of his body, and then settled into a sense of clarity that he had never experienced before. It became apparent to him that his sense of inner feeling was alive and strong, and that, in fact, he could meditate. Feeling through meditation was the perfect place for Charlie to start his practice. Eventually, as he continues to meditate, his other inner senses will be rejuvenated.

When we perceive our world fully through our senses during meditation or waking life, reality is as clear to us as our inner and outer senses are strong. The more fully developed our senses are, the more alive we become. For this reason, we endeavor to exercise them during meditation. The senses that so many of us tend to neglect, ignore, or label *just imagination* are essential to meditation—and life—experience. So let us nurture our senses, in ourselves and in our children. This will enhance our meditative experience and also improve our daily lives by enabling us to have a fuller sensational experience at all times.

chapter 3

VISUAL, AUDITORY, AND
KINESTHETIC LEARNING

THE SENSES ARE OUR VEHICLE FOR LEARNING NEW THINGS. If
we take a tour of a castle, we not only *see* the stone abutments and
the moat, and thereby understand what castle defenses were like,
but we also learn what castles *smell* like through our nostrils. If we
hear someone drop her purse, we learn what dropping something in
a castle sounds like. We might run a hand down the stone wall and
learn about its *texture*.

The senses you use most frequently to absorb information about
the world, and to thereby understand it, are called by some researchers
your *learning style*. Some of us are kinesthetic learners and are most
comfortable learning about the world by touching objects and feeling
emotions; others are auditory learners and absorb information most
easily by hearing words and other sounds; yet others learn best by
analyzing what we see. A child's learning style affects the way he
experiences meditation. Parents and teachers who are familiar with
these learning styles will find it easier to guide children's meditations.
It is important to note that your child's learning style is one with
his meditation experience. That is, his meditation experience is the
totality of his sensations and what he learns from them. We can better
guide our child's meditation experience when we are sensitive to his
ability to feel, hear, and see his world. Additionally, it is important to
understand how *our own* learning style affects our perception of what
meditation is. I will explain this further in this chapter.

SUPPORTING YOUR CHILD'S LEARNING STYLES

If you have used filters on a camera or in a computer graphics program, you know how an image changes based on the filter used to view it. In the same way, our experience changes based on the learning styles we use to make sense of what is happening. The way we perceive our world is filtered through our consciousness via our learning styles. The words we choose to explain our experience are also based on our learning styles.

We learn and process information in three primary ways: visual, auditory, and kinesthetic. A *visual* person easily sees memories in his mind, and says things like "I see what you mean" or "I can picture that." An *auditory* learner benefits from a class lecture, and says things like "I hear what you are saying" or "That sounds good." A *kinesthetic* processor is aware of his feelings about things. He might not necessarily recall the details of an event, but he can remember exactly how the situation made him feel. He might say "I feel good about that" or "I'll touch upon this."

Linda is greatly affected by what she *hears*. She likes music, dislikes banging noises, and uses an auditory learning style most frequently. Auditory learners benefit most from listening to explanations, from music, and from the words and sounds they hear during meditation.

Nico enjoys gazing at beautiful art, and is irritated with the way his matchbox car collection *looks* when it is disorganized. He clearly benefits from visual stimuli. Some children learn best by remembering an idea as a mental image—they lean toward visual learning. It might be easier for these children to recall information by thinking about how the object looked and enjoy the images they see during meditation.

Maria yearns for a back massage, and avoids heights because they make her *feel* uncomfortable. She uses her kinesthetic abilities most often to learn about the world around her. A kinesthetic child learns a great deal by physically touching the object being studied, and such children can better tell you about their meditation when they remember how they felt while meditating.

Again, although we might have a tendency to use a certain learning style most often, we all process information audibly, visually and kinesthetically. When guiding your child through a meditation, your understanding of these three learning styles can help you inspire him. Although knowing his learning style helps you use effective words to enhance a child's meditation experience, it is always best to consciously incorporate all three approaches so he can have a fuller sensual experience and practice all styles of learning. This point is important: focus the meditative exercise in the way that best suits your child's primary learning style, but don't exclude the other learning styles.

Here are some ways you can support *visual* learning.

~ When introducing a new concept, use a picture to show what you are talking about. When I teach children about moving energy through their bodies, I use a large wooden board cut in the shape of a life-sized torso and head, decorated with the seven chakras. All the children who see this visual representation better understand where the chakras are located, but visual learners really respond. The kinesthetic learners might touch each chakra point on their own bodies, and the auditory learners need only hear about the locations of the chakras, but the visual learner thrives on this kind of demonstration.

~ Chapter 5 suggests that after meditation you give your child an art project. Art activities help children create visual images of feelings and concepts. A picture is worth a thousand words, as the saying goes, so look carefully at your child's picture to see the words and feelings he is expressing, especially if he is a visual learner. Art exercises also strengthen the visual sense in children with primarily auditory and kinesthetic learning styles.

~ When working with your child to establish personal goals, help him create a collage of pictures representing a particular goal or dream. Or lead him through a meditation in which he visualizes his goals being met.

~ To help your child improve his relationships, have him close his eyes and visualize resolving any conflict he is having with another person. For example, ten-year-old, Noah might, during meditation, watch himself ask his sister to please stop taking his toys out of his room.

The following points describe supports for *auditory* learning.

~ Children who are auditory benefit from the spoken word. Speak clearly and directly about the topic.

~ Play music during a meditation session or art activity. Sing songs about meditation (see the activities at the ends of chapters 8, 9, 10, and 11).

~ Guide your child to hear things during meditation. Afterward, ask him what sounds he heard. For example, if he released energies down his grounding cord, ask him, "What did it sound like when stuff was moving through your grounding cord?" Again, these exercises best serve auditory learners, but children who learn primarily by touching and feeling or seeing can enhance their ability to learn auditorily with these approaches.

The following are ways to help your child get in touch with feelings during meditation time, which supports *kinesthetic* learning.

~ Art activities cater to the kinesthetic child. Do projects that involve touching the medium, such as finger painting and handling clay. Art helps raise any child's self-esteem and opens a strong channel for expression, especially in kinesthetic learners.

~ When teaching your child about auras, show him how to feel his own aura. For a step-by-step description of this activity, see Chapter 9.

~ In meditation we often receive information intuitively. Sometimes children are not sure whether to trust this kind of information. Ask your child what he feels in his body when he thinks about something he has intuited. If he feels warm in his heart (or experiences another positive feeling), he should know he can trust it. You can also encourage non-kinesthetic meditators to explore their feelings by asking them to associate a sensation with an emotion. This exercise can enhance the ability of non-kinesthetic learners to get in touch with their emotions. This can be especially useful for a child whose primary faculty is reason. Being able to solve problems using reason is a good attribute, obviously, but intuition, going with one's gut feeling, can certainly be useful, too.

HOW YOUR LEARNING STYLES AFFECT YOUR CHILD'S MEDITATION

The learning styles your child uses affect the way he communicates his experience. For example, Ruby tells her mother about the *tickle* she felt in her heart during meditation and the *tingling* in her feet at the end. The way we adults communicate is also affected by the learning styles we use. When you guide your child through a meditation adventure, your own learning style affects the words you choose to lead him.

If you are predominantly visual, you might use words like *see* and *look*. When giving instructions you are apt to say something like, "See the tree. Notice the colors." When you become aware of your tendencies, you will know to add, "Notice what the tree sounds like. Do you hear birds, or wind?" and "Notice how you feel when you look at the tree." This will open up your child's experience, allowing him to experiment with all three learning styles during meditation.

I like to use all three forms of sensation in equal measure as much as possible when I lead groups of children. Sometimes when I work with a child privately for a few sessions, I find out what learning style he prefers. I ask him whether it is more fun for him to *look* at the tree in his mind, to *hear* the sounds it made, or to *feel* feelings in his body. Then, to facilitate his enjoyment of the experience, I might favor one learning style over the others when I guide him through meditation. I do not totally exclude the other modalities, however.

If you are not sure what learning styles you use most frequently, notice what words you use the next time you describe a person, place, or object to someone. Are these words visually descriptive; do they reference sounds or conversations; or do they explain feelings (emotional and physical)? The following exercise will help you determine your primary and secondary learning styles. Keep in mind that we all process information audibly, visually, *and* kinesthetically; however, we typically use one style more frequently. The style we choose also depends on the situation, of course. For example, you might favor visual abilities when it comes to a neat house but favor feelings when you go dancing. In general, however, most of us favor one style over the others.

EXERCISE 3

What Are My Learning Styles?

As I stated earlier, our personal learning styles greatly affect the words we use to lead children in meditation. This, in turn, greatly affects the child's meditation experience. Use the following test to determine your primary and secondary learning styles. Then use this awareness to better understand your own meditation experience and your influence on your child's meditation experience.

Don't spend too much time choosing your answers.

1. If I need to teach myself how to use my new camera, I prefer to
   a) Watch a video about it.
   b) Listen to someone explain it.
   c) Begin using it on my own and learn as I go.

2. When I meet new people, I remember
   a) Their faces but not always their names.
   b) Their names but not their faces.
   c) The emotions that came up while talking to the person.

3. When I hear or read the name of someone, I instantly
   a) Remember what this person looks like.
   b) Say the name silently in my mind.
   c) Remember the feeling of being with this person.

4. When I have a magazine, I would rather
   a) Flip through the magazine and look at the pictures.
   b) Find a good interview with someone and read it.
   c) Find a self-test or puzzle and do that.

5. When I have trouble spelling a word, I
   a) Write it out until it looks correct.
   b) Speak the word aloud or in my head.
   c) Notice how it feels when I write it.

6. If I wanted to make some home improvements, I would first

    a) Make drawings of what I want to do.

    b) Talk to people who could tell me what to do.

    c) Start moving things around, work with the tools, and plan as I go.

7. When studying for a test, what works best for me is

    a) Reading over my notes and the text, and looking over any pictures that explain the material.

    b) Repeating the important information aloud or silently to myself.

    c) Writing out the important information and drawing diagrams.

8. What distracts me the most is

    a) Flashing lights.

    b) Loud noises.

    c) Sensations in my body.

9. At a petting zoo, I am most interested in

    a) Observing the animals.

    b) Listening to zoo employees tell me about the animals.

    c) Touching the animals.

10. If I won the lottery, I would instantly

    a) Smile and see images of what I would do with the money.

    b) Scream for joy.

    c) Jump up and down.

I had _____ As.

I had _____ Bs.

I had _____ Cs.

As you probably already figured out, *A*s are associated with visual learning, *B*s with auditory learning, and *C*s with kinesthetic learning. The letter you selected most often is the learning type you probably use most often. If one letter does not stand out more than the others, you might have two dominant learning types, or equal types. Most people have a dominant learning style and a secondary one that they also use frequently. Remember we all differ, and someone who learns one way is not inferior to someone who learns another way.

I invite you to observe how your learning style plays an important role in your life. You might also choose to experiment with the learning styles you do not favor, to expand your sensual experience during meditation and in daily life.

chapter 4

MINDFULNESS FOR CHILDREN

George, a mindfulness teacher for children, places a large standing bell (singing bowl) made of glass and two smaller standing bells in front of his students. Pointing to the glass bell, George asks, "Can anyone guess what this is?"

After revealing that the round and smooth object is a *bell*, George asks his students which bell they think will ring a lower pitch and which one a higher pitch. Next, George instructs his students to listen closely to the bell. After the last vibrations of the bell are heard, he asks the children to describe what the ringing sounded like.

The following week, George invites his students to listen to surrounding sounds, such as movement in the room, chatter in the hallway, and noises outdoors, while the bell rings.

"Did you hear the buzz of the florescent lights in the room?" George asks. "Did you hear the helicopter outside? How quiet do we have to be to hear these things?"

"Really quiet," the students respond.

To help his students develop more mindfulness, George next asks his students to choose one object to look at more deeply than usual. Again, he instructs the children to notice these details while the bell rings.

"I saw a fly land on my knee," one boy shares afterwards. "I could see the veins in the fly's wings."

Over time, George's students learn how to still their bodies and stay alert so they can better notice the world around them. This practice is referred to as *mindfulness.*

George's students sometimes feel a deep moment of stillness after their mindfulness exercises. The children describe this tranquility as similar to flying or being on a cloud. Inevitably, some students report that they feel bored when they practice mindfulness. However, George does not discount answers such as "boring" in reference to this stillness because he models non-judgment and knows that his students are simply learning to observe. If "boring" is what his students noticed, then these students have observed perfectly.

DEFINITION OF MINDFULNESS

Jon Kabat-Zinn, famous for bringing the concept of mindfulness to mainstream America, defines *mindfulness* as purposefully paying attention to the present moment, without judgment.

Mindfulness is rooted in Buddhist practice. In fact, mindfulness is one of the *Seven Factors of Enlightenment* that Buddha taught to help his students move towards enlightenment. For this reason, I consider mindfulness to be one piece of the "meditation pie" and maintain an understanding that other elements contribute to our overall practice. For example, stilling the body helps us be more mindful, yet this action is not mindfulness. Additionally, the act of concentration is essential to successful mindfulness practice, yet it is not mindfulness.

With that being said, mindfulness is more than sitting in meditation. Mindfulness can be practiced while walking, eating, or during most any activity we perform. Mindfulness can be practiced while sitting still and staring at a rock as we notice each grove in its surface, for instance. Mindfulness can also mean saying to ourselves when we get angry with a sibling, "I am really angry right now," instead of reacting physically. And this practice can also mean letting go of every story we have made up in our heads about failing, so that we may better perform on an upcoming test.

Therefore, when we introduce mindfulness to children, we can guide children to evolve their own definition of *mindfulness*, in the same way we support children to come up with their own meaning of *meditation*. In doing so, the child feels a sense of ownership for her practice, personalizes it, and, therefore, will hopefully be more inclined to practice on her own.

BENEFITS OF MINDFULNESS

Mindfulness helps us distinguish between what is real and what is not real. In the context of mindfulness, consider this example. We sit on our porch and listen to the birds chirp. Then we begin to think about the laundry we left unfolded in the house. And then we worry about a meeting we attended the day before. The birds' chirping is *real* because it occurs in the present moment. However, most mindfulness instructors would say that folding the laundry and the meeting are *not real* because they are based on possibilities dangling in the future or events that took place in the past. Therefore, I invite you to deem, in light of mindfulness, that neither the past nor the future is real. Hence, what is happening right now becomes more important than what has already taken place and more significant than future possibilities.

When children *keep it real*, they improve their attention and focus because they are not distracted by what is not real—the past and the future. Moreover, when children learn how to guide their minds to settle on what is happening right now, they build healthy relationships with their peers. This is because they do not make decisions about how to treat their peers based on old events or thoughts about what might happen in the future—the *what ifs*.

School administrators across the globe are pleasantly surprised by the positive effects of mindfulness. These administrators observe less conflict and better focus on academics. Furthermore, many psychologists teach mindfulness to their clients to alleviate a variety of mental and physical conditions, including obsessive-compulsive disorder, anxiety, depression, and drug addiction.

One study, which included both adults and adolescents diagnosed with Attention Deficit Hyperactivity Disorder (ADHD), found that 78% of subjects reduced their ADHD symptoms after learning and practicing mindfulness techniques focused on the breath. The subjects participated in seven two-and-a-half-hour training sessions[1].

Another mindfulness study showed that children were more likely to make decisions based on their own ideas after learning mindfulness (sitting and paying attention to their breathing). This characteristic, making decisions based on their own ideas, is referred to as *field-independence* and linked to better overall academic performance. In this study, child subjects practiced mindfulness mediation two times per week for eighteen weeks. Children significantly reduced their test anxiety during this study.[2]

TIPS FOR TEACHING MINDFULNESS FOR CHILDREN

Although most Buddhists will not come out and articulate that the goal of mindfulness is to reduce the number of thoughts running through our minds, I am going to give my readers a jump start and proclaim that *cleaning house* is indeed the reason we practice mindfulness. When we think less, we have less to fight about, less to stress about, and less to distract us from the task at hand.

Thinking less does not mean we walk around like zombies—quite the opposite. In this state of heightened awareness, we naturally react to situations with, what Buddhists term, more *skill*. With skillful thought, skillful speech, and skillful action, we form healthier bonds with others and make life choices that serve us better.

If mindfulness is a practice that helps us reduce the number of thoughts we think, then *why do we think so many thoughts in the first place?* When I began to consider this question years ago, I decided there must be a logical reason as to why humans are such head cases.

After meditating on the question for some time, I came to realize that we think so we can keep our bodies and emotional beings safe.

If a bus is headed straight for us, it certainly helps to assess the situation and think, *I should move out of the street so I don't get run over.* I would even go as far as to say that our Creator sent us into this world with a built-in simulator, which we can use to toss ideas around within and come up with possible outcomes. *If I keep standing here, I will get run over* is one possibility that comes out of the simulator at lightening speed.

The bus scenario is a great example of when to use the simulator. In this case, it helps us keep our bodies safe. However, during a typical day we spend way too much time in the simulator. In other words, we use analytical thought far too often. For example, we do not need to use the simulator to rehash our last conversation with our mother-in-law. Perhaps we spend only five minutes analyzing the conversation and then we let it go so that we may listen to the birds chirping outside. Any practice that helps us decrease our dependency on analytical thought is helpful. (Some mindfulness teachers instruct us to notice the repetitive thoughts and allow these thoughts to dissipate naturally, as opposed to shifting attention to sounds or our breath.)

Here are some tips to help introduce mindfulness to children:

Tip #1 Promise Safety: Consider the notion, *thoughts keep us safe.* The first step in teaching mindfulness to a child is to reassure her that she will be protected during her practice with you. A young child whose parents ensure that she is safe may not need your reassurance as much as another child who lacks such parental support. A child who literally experiences physical danger on a repetitive basis or is vulnerable to insult (emotional and mental danger) will highly benefit from hearing that she will be safe while she meditates—safe to stop thinking, even if just for a moment.

There are many children who fall in between these two extremes—almost always safe and rarely safe. Use your best judgment to determine how much emphasis you should place on letting the child know that you will see to it that no other students invade her physical space or say negative things about her while you lead her through meditation.

Tip #2 Engage All of the Senses: George asked his students to notice sounds, sights, and feelings while his bell rung. Mindfulness exercises can also involve paying attention to our breath or other physical sensations that engage our senses. Please note, this practice of awareness can take place while a bell rings or in silence.

The following are sensations that your child can focus on during mindfulness meditation:

Hearing: ringing bell, birds, sound of breath, music

Sight: eyes open - plant, rock, rising and falling chest while breathing; eyes closed - imaginary pictures in head, back of eyelids

Touch/emotions: texture of skin on hands, texture of item in hand, air in nostrils while breathing, feelings such as happiness, sadness, and excitement

Taste: natural taste in mouth, taste after eating sweet, salty, or sour item(s)

Smell: natural scent in room, essential oils, flowers, candle

Tip #3 Facilitate Supporting Activities: In addition to the meditations offered in Chapter 8, the following are ways you can support a child to better understand the intricacies of mindfulness and deepen her mindfulness practice.

• Show the child a picture and ask her to study it carefully for one minute. Then take the picture away and ask her specific questions about the picture, such as, "What color was the flower in the picture?" Or, ask open-ended questions, such as, "What can you tell me about what you remember from the picture?" The child will need to be mindful while observing the picture to remember these details.

• Ask the child to keep a journal of what she did during the day. This helps the child be mindful of what actions she took. Eventually, she can then note what feelings she felt and what thoughts she thought at different points in her day to deepen her level of mindfulness. (This involves past events, which are not objects of mindfulness, however the activity is good practice for the child.)

• Help the child notice her emotions. For example, play a song and ask her to notice how she feels while the song plays. She might become mindful of excitement or sleepiness, or she might feel like a cloud floating in the sky.

Tip # 4 Encourage Evolving Definition of Mindfulness: Offer your opinions and experiences about your personal mindfulness practice. However, as discussed earlier, create a space for your child to come up with her own definition of mindfulness.

Tip #5 Encourage Children to Keep a Record of Improvement: The most popular reason for continuing a mindfulness practice is creating a better life. In other words, meditators do not necessarily maintain a good mindfulness practice because they love how they feel during meditation (although some do). The motivation, for many of us, is more about how we feel later in the day.

Many of the meditations in this book are fun and provide an inner adventure that kids love. Mindfulness meditation, on the other hand, can be boring for some children. Simply sitting or lying down for several minutes to enjoy the relaxation benefits of mindfulness is enough to motivate some children to continue; however, for other children, an awareness of how their practice helps them in their everyday life is sometimes more encouraging.

Your child can document her success by drawing pictures, writing in a journal, or both. This process of documenting her success and looking at it later helps her realize how valuable her mindfulness practice is. As an alternative to a journal, keep a video documentary of her response to her personal practice by interviewing her on video every week or so. Ask questions such as, "Did you do anything this week in a more mindful way?" or "Did you notice feeling better about taking your test this week?" or "Do you think your mindfulness meditation made _____ easier for you?" Remember to make it fun!

Mindfulness meditations are provided in Chapter 8.

chapter 5

TIPS FOR SUCCESS

MEDITATION EMPOWERS US TO FIND THE HAPPINESS we naturally strive for, however; the *way* we are taught to meditate also empowers us. The elements of my approach to teaching, parenting, and meditation sprout from one single intention: to empower children to be happy and fully alive human beings.

This chapter shares six important tips that will help you successfully give the gift of a meditation practice to your child. Although they are presented to help you teach your child how to meditate, you will find that children are naturally good meditators. Many adults are skeptical about a child's ability to meditate because many adults find it difficult to sit down and focus. But children love meditation—it allows them to use their creative imaginations without limitation. Although they might be sitting still, their minds are in Technicolor overdrive at a level many grownups have forgotten is possible.

Children do not require a dark, quiet room or a place free from distractions when they meditate. Children can easily jump into and out of meditation when something interrupts them. Much of this ability is due to their brainwave state: children naturally exist in a meditative state.

Our brains emit waves that can be detected and measured. The slowest detected waves are delta waves (4 cycles per second). We experience this wave pattern when we are sleeping or in a deep hypnotic state.[1] Interestingly, children from birth to two years old spend most of their time in this state. As a child matures, these waves gradually quicken. Between two and six years of age, children spend much of their time in a theta state (4 to 8 cycles per second). This is a calm, meditative state when the analytical mind is at rest. Later, a child's brain wave pattern increases to the alpha state (8 to 12 cycles per second). In this state we are quiet, yet open to the workings of the world. Eventually, in adolescence, a child moves into the beta state (12 to 35 cycles per second). This is a state that lends itself well to analytical tasks, and is the state that most of us settle into in adulthood.

Many postulate that the reason infants' and children's brains function in slower brain wave states is because they have so very much to learn about their world. If they were to analyze everything that came into their experience they would be overwhelmed and might not even be able to function. Instead, for example, infants remain in a deep meditative delta state that allows information to stream through their senses and settle into their subconscious.

As adults we may have difficulty accessing our inner mind to experience the images, sounds, and feelings that arise in meditation. Society puts a premium on a certain kind of rational intelligence, at the cost of imagination and creativity. Children, on the other hand, are by nature imaginative, and happily use their inner and outer senses to explore their inner and outer worlds. I find in general that the children I teach are far more open to the practice than my adult students. They grasp far more easily that a feeling can have color or that they can taste something without ever putting it into their mouths, because their imaginations allow for such experiences in their everyday world. They don't have to be told that they can feel energy flowing through their bodies; they know this already. They are aware of the life energy pulsing within them.

TIP 1: KEEP YOUR DEFINITION OF MEDITATION SIMPLE AND OPEN

Kahlil Gibran, a beloved, Near East poet, philosopher and artist, writes a poem about children, in his book *The Prophet*.[2] He says,

"You may give them your love but not your thoughts,
For they have their own thoughts."

Can we teach a spiritual practice or a set of skills to children without shaping their thoughts? I believe we can if we *consciously* introduce concepts to children. Previous chapters discuss the *six dimensions of consciousness* and learning styles. Later chapters cover how to let thoughts pass through our consciousness, dichotomies and past lives. You might agree with the way I present these ideas, but your child might not. If she does agree, she might discover a deeper layer of clarity that we, as teachers and parents, could not have anticipated. I discuss these topics so that you have a solid foundation for presenting the meditations to your child. This foundation, for the most part, is meant to help answer children's questions instead of providing additional curriculum for your child.

Gibran continues his beliefs on children,

"You may strive to be like them,

but seek not to make them like you.

For life goes not backward nor tarries with yesterday."

Our job is to focus on facilitating experiences for our children and letting them draw their own conclusions. One way to avoid shaping your students' thinking is this: Do not give an absolute definition of meditation. Empower them to decide. In the same way, create a definition for yourself as well. Once you feel good about your understanding of meditation, you can help your child develop her own. You and your child learn together and from one another. Together you discover what meditation means in your lives.

Regarding younger students, refrain from *teaching* them about meditation. Instead show them the relevance, context and usefulness of the meditations and activities you offer. (In chapters 8, 9, 10, and 11, before each meditation, you'll see a description of how the mediation helps the child.) As children grow older and gain a better sense of the difference between *your beliefs* and *their beliefs*, bring some of these concepts into discussions. In groups of children who vary in ages, use your best judgment. In all circumstances, remember that you own your beliefs about how the universe works. You create space for your students to form their own conclusions as well.

Meditation is a relatively big word for most children, and indeed, defining meditation can be intimidating even when explaining it to an adult. One simple definition of meditation is *experiencing our inner and outer worlds, usually with our eyes closed.* When I talk to children, I often describe meditation as *seeing, hearing, and feeling our world with our eyes closed.* I also tell them that when we meditate, we can practice actions or feelings in our heads so that we can do them easily later on. I offer an easy example: if you do not know how to ride a bike, seeing yourself ride a bike in your mind will help you learn. Then I might up the ante a bit and offer a more abstract example, one that has emotional and psychological implications. I might say, "When you practice how to let go of angry energy in your body during meditation, you can more easily let go of your anger when you feel it after meditating." Then I may suggest an even larger concept: meditation can help you understand yourself better. This idea always elicits *oohs* and *ahhs* and some excellent questions.

Older children respond to definitions like we are creating a connection to a divine source, experiencing inner silence, or using metaphoric journey to heal and understand ourselves better.

Before you attempt to convey to your child what meditation is, I invite you to explore your own personal definition.

EXERCISE 4

How Do I Define Meditation?

Remember that there is no absolutely right way to define meditation. The first step is to have your own definition.

Once you have it, translate it into simple language that your child can relate to, using your knowledge of who your child is and how she perceives the world to help you choose the right words.

Consider the following questions while forming your definition, especially if you are new to meditation.

Why do I meditate?

What do I feel when I meditate?

How do I position my body?

What is my mind doing while I meditate?

How does meditation help people?

If you are new to meditation, the answers may not come easy. But just giving them a try will help you formulate a definition that your child can understand. When you are ready to share it with your child, stress that this is what meditation means to you, and keep it simple. Encourage your child to create her own definition when she is ready. This enhances her sense of herself and her practice; she realizes she has the *power* to define it.

If you are considering discussing meditation with your child's teachers or school administrator, remember that not everyone is entirely open to meditation. Although many spiritual traditions practice some form of meditation, some people believe that it conflicts with their religious views, or they simply do not know enough about it to feel comfortable with it. If you use other terminology, however, such as creative visualization, guided visualization, concentration exercises, relaxation exercises, closed-eye processing, inner processing, or mindfulness skills, your audience may be more open and accepting.

TIP 2: DEMONSTRATE HOW EASY MEDITATION IS

Meditation is not complicated or difficult. It does not require years of practice. It is very natural, and it is fun! Anyone can be a marvelous meditator even if she has just begun. Still, we may place obstacles in the way of our practice because we believe that it is difficult. It is possible that you might transfer this belief to your child, in which case performance anxiety could be her initial reaction (and you might experience this yourself).

Premeditation Jitters

When I work with beginning students, whether children or adults, I start with a visualization exercise that quickly demonstrates how simple it is to meditate. I explain that meditation is as easy as closing our eyes, thinking about an object, and then seeing a picture of it in our minds. The following exercise can dismiss any fears you or your child might have about not being able to meditate.

EXERCISE

Seeing Pictures in Our Heads

1. First, tell your child to close her eyes and think of what her bedroom looks like.

2. Then ask her to imagine her bed, the pictures hanging on the walls, her toys, and so on. If you are working with a group of children, ask them to raise their hands when they can see their bedrooms so you know when everyone has done so. If there is anyone who is not able to see an image of her bedroom, assist her further. For example, invite her to get a feeling for what is in her room, or ask her to pretend to listen to something in her room.

3. When your child has seen a picture in her mind, ask her to open her eyes.

After performing this exercise, ask, "If your eyes were closed when you saw the picture of your bedroom, then how did you see it?" This leads to interesting conversation about inner vision. Exploring how we can see pictures in our heads with our eyes closed instantly demonstrates the power of our inner senses. As I said previously, children are usually already aware of this fabulous ability, but even those with the most magnificent imaginations have rarely had the opportunity to identify the part of themselves that has inner vision. Each child will come up with her own unique explanation, and each explanation is as valid as the next as the children explore their imaginative abilities and search for words to define this experience.

Tip 3: Encourage Your Child to Choose Her Own Meditation Posture

We can meditate sitting in a chair, lying down, or sitting cross-legged on the floor. Before leading your child through her first few meditations, mention and demonstrate various relaxing ways she can position her body during the meditation, letting her know it doesn't matter which way she chooses, as long as she is comfortable. Encourage your child to close her eyes. Explain that placing her hands over her eyes makes keeping them closed easier. Even after years of meditation, I frequently hold my hands over my eyes while meditating because the light often interferes with my concentration.

At some point, suggest that your child set up a special meditation place in your home so that some private space can be associated with the practice. Remind her, too, that she can meditate anywhere: on a bus, on a swing, under a tree, or in a classroom. The world is our meditation place. We can even meditate with our eyes open. Knowing this, your child will view meditation as a tool she carries with her rather than something she can only do under ideal circumstances.

Sarah Tower, child relaxation teacher mentioned in Chapter 1, says yoga mats are one of her best-kept secrets. Children know where their space is and, for the most part, enjoy staying in their special space. Sarah reminds fidgeting children to take deep breaths.

Tip 4: Avoid Rules and Restrictions

In Chapters 8 through 11, I offer 12 meditations that last between 5 and 10 minutes, which is a good length of time for children. Children move quickly through the imagery, their emotions, and the words and sounds. They experience much in a short span of time, while an adult meditator might take longer to achieve the same result, or might linger for the sheer joy of the experience. Observe your child's interest in the experience to determine if you should slow down or speed up the meditation.

If your child opens her eyes and looks around during meditation, it's fine. Simply encourage her to cover her eyes. She may speak aloud; this will not interfere with the flow of meditation. It probably will not affect other children's focus, either, if kept to a minimum. If your child asks questions, softly reply. When she makes simple comments or observations, let it become a part of the experience. Just let it go.

Although a certain level of quiet is necessary for meditation, this level is different for children. Strict guidelines and discipline will make it hard for your child to meditate. She is engaged in an act of deep consciousness; demanding absolute stillness is both unrealistic and an invitation for her to associate this extraordinary experience with some less gratifying event. The fewer rules and restrictions you set, the more enlightening meditation will be, and the more forthcoming your child will be with her experiences afterward.

Sarah, as mentioned earlier, also suggests that students make up their own story or simply listen to the music if they are not interested in the meditation. She reassures her students that this is their time to relax and how they choose do so is up to them.

TIP 5: INVITE YOUR CHILD TO TALK ABOUT HER MEDITATION EXPERIENCES

Provide your child with space and time to talk about her experiences. When she has a chance to articulate her abstract thoughts, she can understand more clearly what she has experienced. At the same time, when you share images, sounds, and feelings *you* have during meditation, your child will gain from your perspective.

This is especially valuable in groups because so much can be learned from hearing what others see, feel, and understand. A child who hears another child's vision of colored beams of light, angels, or animal guides knows she can experience these energies in her next meditation. You can also help her to recognize that her experiences are by no means out of the ordinary; they are valid and can be explored more deeply.

When a child relates the story of her meditation journey, she reveals how she experiences the world, and when we understand how our children experience the world, we can help them find peace in it. The "Time Machine" meditation in Chapter 11 reveals how your child views her future and the world's future. "The Happy Tree" meditation, also in Chapter 11, helps both you and your child understand what actions to take to help her out of her sadness.

When a child shares what she experiences during meditation, you might notice a pattern to the symbolism her subconscious uses to express particular ideas. Teaching children about symbolism can be challenging because children are literalists: what they think and what they perceive is exactly that and not some abstraction in need of interpretation. Nevertheless, delving into this subject can help your child to connect what she sees in meditation with her life. Some children can see the psychological and emotional meaning within the images, sounds, and feelings. Their perception will lead to a deeper understanding of themselves. For others, however, such interpretations will diminish the mystery of their adventure and detract from their exciting world of talking trees and flying peanuts.

You can let your child determine whether her meditation images were real or symbolic simply by asking questions like the following: "Do you think the picture you saw means something?" "Do you think of anything else when you see your grandmother in meditation?" If the child is very young, she will describe the image as exactly what it was: a feeling or a sound. But if she is ready for further interpretation, you may talk to her about symbolism. If you feel there is an advantage in introducing this facet of meditation, the following demonstrates how to take this next step.

Teaching Symbolism to Children

1. Begin by asking your child, "Do you know what a *symbol* is?" Some children might know that a *cymbal* is a type of musical instrument, but most will not know the word as you are using it. In this case, share the meaning of *symbol* in language that she can understand, and use a common example from her daily life. For example, "A symbol is a picture that means something. A picture of a dog with a circle around it and a red line through the center is a symbol for No Dogs Allowed. When we meditate, the pictures we see can also represent something else."

   Although symbolism is usually thought of as visual, symbolic elements in meditation can also be heard or felt. For example, the sound of a pounding drum could represent pain.

2. Share a personal experience—something symbolic you saw, heard, or felt in meditation that meant something to you. Maybe you saw a butterfly come out of a cocoon, which you took to mean that you are growing into a new way of being, or maybe you heard a song that meant something special to you. If you are not an experienced meditator, you might have to think about this a bit. Choose an example that is relatively easy for a child to understand. For example, the image of a butterfly emerging from a chrysalis would be easy to explain and easy for your child to grasp.

3. Ask your child if she has ever seen a symbol in her head, either during a meditation, in a dream, or at any other time. Be completely open to what your child shares with you. You will probably hear a wide range of responses. Then ask her what she thinks this image, sound, or feeling represents. Again, empower your child to interpret her own symbolism instead of interpreting it for her. In time, your child will surprise you with the accuracy of her interpretations, and probably she'll eventually delight you by trumping what you thought the image meant for her.

TIP 6: OFFER CREATIVE PROJECTS TO SUPPORT YOUR CHILD'S MEDITATION

Art, writing, and music are effective ways for a child to integrate meditation into her world. Creative projects allow children to hold the memory of a meditation in their consciousness, and examine and reflect on its different facets. They have many *ah-ha!* moments in the process. Consider the following.

Amy notices that her daughter Ashley is depressed. Amy decides to facilitate "The Happy Tree" meditation with Ashley because it is supposed to help relieve sadness. During meditation, Ashley sees a tree with happy and sad apples. On one of her sad apples she sees the face of her good friend Tamari, who moved away. On her happy apples she sees the sun, a rainbow, and smiley faces.

When Ashley opens her eyes after meditation, she remembers the sun, rainbow, and smiley faces but forgets the vision of her friend. Later, while drawing a picture of the tree that she saw during meditation, she remembers the vision of her friend and is inspired to include a drawing of Tamari in her picture. Ashley tells her mother the story about her good friend who moved away, and explains that this is why some of her fruits were sad. Now for the first time, Ashley and her mother know why Ashley has been depressed. Afterward, Amy helps her daughter write a letter to Tamari.

Each of the meditations discussed in Chapters 8 through 11 includes an art project your child can enjoy after meditating. Writing and music activities are also great ways to help your child remember and integrate details of her meditation.

Sample Meditation Time Outline

You might consider introducing your child to *Meditation Time*, a special time for you and your child to meditate, to talk, and to share other activities like art and music. A clear outline for your Meditation Time with your child is provided here. This outline can also be used to facilitate a meditation class for a group of children. These directions include the six tips I've discussed, in addition to some new suggestions for steps two and eight.

Review of the Six Tips

1. Keep Your Definition of Meditation Simple and Open
2. Demonstrate How Easy Meditation Is
3. Encourage Your Child to Choose Her Own Meditation Posture
4. Avoid Rules and Restrictions
5. Invite Your Child to Talk About Her Meditation Experiences
6. Offer Creative Projects to Support Your Child's Meditation

Meditation Time

1. **Checking In.** Begin by asking your child how she's feeling and what's been on her mind.

   If you are working with a group of students, first introduce yourself and have all the students introduce themselves. This will facilitate open discussion and sharing. Ask the children to tell you their names and possibly their ages. Asking for more information in the beginning can intimidate them; but later, when they feel more comfortable, the students will share more about themselves. Next, ask how each child is feeling at the outset of a meditation session. This step can bring useful information about the child's life to your attention, and you can design specific meditations aimed at a particular child's needs.

2. **Fun Activity.** Believe it or not, your child might think Meditation Time is boring. You can dispel any preconceived notions that your time together will not be interesting by kicking off with a fun activity. For example, you can do the "Let Go Hokey Pokey" (see Chapter 8).

3. **Let's Talk About the Word** *Meditation.* Ask your child what *meditation* means for her, especially if you are in your first few months of meditating together. Explain that no answer is wrong, that we all have our own ideas about what this word means, and that you are particularly interested in what she thinks and feels about the practice. After your child has told you her definition, share your own. It is important to reiterate that it is fine if her definition is different in some respects from yours.

4. **Seeing Pictures in Our Head.** Use the following activity to diffuse any fears your child might have about not being able to meditate, especially if you are in your first few months of meditating together. This exercise will also inspire children to think about their *third eye,* or intuitive center. Ask your child to close her eyes and imagine what her bedroom looks like. Guide her to see her bed, walls, toys, books, and other objects in her room. When she has seen an image in her mind, tell her to open her eyes. If working with a group, first find out if anyone is unable to see their bedroom. Help students who are having difficulty. Then ask, "Since your eyes were closed, how did you see the picture of your bedroom?" This is a turning point of understanding for most children because they realize we have a way to *see* without using our eyes. If you will be leading

your child through a mindfulness meditation such as "Me and My Zen," you might replace this exercise with a shortened version of the "Mindfulness" meditation in Chapter 8

5. **Special Topic.** Before going into the meditation, you might consider discussing the topic of your meditation. This is a time to ask questions designed to inspire your child or students to think about the concepts you are teaching. This is not, however, a time to go into formal definitions about your subject. It is better to save these for afterward. After her meditation experience your child will have a frame of reference, and your formal definitions will be grounded in her experiences.

6. **Encourage Your Child to Choose Her Own Meditation Posture.** Talk about various body positions your child can use when meditating, and practice them if you wish. Also mention that it will be easier for your child to keep her eyes closed if she covers them with her hands.

7. **The Meditation.** Read the meditation instructions you have chosen or prepared beforehand. Or let the meditation come forth spontaneously, possibly based upon the meditation creation methods offered in Chapter 12. Remember to avoid rules and restrictions whenever possible.

8. **Invite Your Child to Talk About Her Meditation Experiences.** After meditation, ask your child if she would like to share what she saw and experienced. You can help by asking such questions as "What did your grounding cord look like?" or "What did your sad fruit need to be happy?" In a group setting, students learn a great deal from hearing their classmates' experiences. If children speak softly, clearly repeat what they say so everyone can benefit from what the others share. For example, "Joe said he saw a bright green light coming out from the top of his head."

9. **"What Did We Do That For?" and Formal Explanation.** Now

that your child has experienced the meditation, explain its purpose if you wish. This is the time to talk about the formal definitions of the concepts you are teaching. I often skip formal definitions all together and trust the children will come to their own conclusions. I do always follow the next step, however.

After meditation, ask your child when she could use this meditation in the future. Try to get a specific answer. If your child offers something like "I would use this meditation next time I get upset," encourage her to think of a particular moment when she gets upset. She might then add, "When I get into a fight with my brother." Doing this extra step helps her see the practicality of the meditation.

10. **Offer a Creative Project to Support Your Child's Meditation.** Offer crayons, markers, and paper, and ask your child to draw something she saw during meditation. Or choose from the many art projects provided in this book. If your child is older than 10, you might also encourage her to write down the steps of the meditation so she can do it later on her own. If you are teaching a class of children, give parents a printed copy of the meditation so they can practice the same meditation with their children.

chapter 6

EVERY CHILD IS UNIQUE

UNDERSTANDING YOUR CHILD IS ESSENTIAL to teaching him meditation. Each child is unique, and behaviors vary in every child from one minute to the next. Consequently, we need to become deeply familiar with the child we are working with: his likes and dislikes, and his behaviors. We also need to create a space for him to be whomever he chooses in any particular moment. In this way, we allow him to use all ten senses, to express himself freely, and to access his highest potential.

Children are sensational beings naturally. They are curious sponges soaking up the world through their eyes, ears, and noses. They use their hands to touch things. They conduct experiments with dirt, paint, food, and just about anything they can reach. These little scientists even use their taste buds to help them open up to the world around them.

When children experience the world through their senses they react to it. A child's behavior is his response to the stimulation that enters through his ten senses. Each child is unique in response to the world. Meditation guides need to take this wonderful fact into account when facilitating meditations and interpreting responses, as well as throughout the day.

Some children are shy while others are social; some are calm and others are active; and the same child can be shy, social, calm, and active depending on the moment. Exploring the uncountable behaviors children use to respond to the world and applying this insight to a child's environment is a wonderful gift to give a child. When you begin to understand your child, you can make adjustments in his environment that will help him. Becoming more conscious of how you interact with him will benefit both him and you. Sometimes we just need to get out of a child's way and allow him to have a full sensational learning experience. Other times our involvement—introducing new ideas and activities—can really help him.

WORKING WITH CHILDREN WHO EXPERIMENT WITH CREATIVITY, HIGH ENERGY, NONCONFORMITY, SENSITIVITY, AND INTUITION

Different energies exist in all of us—energies that are dynamic and a natural part of being alive. I've listed a few here that you may notice in yourself, and in your child as he experiments with life.

~ A *creative* child finds joy when let loose with an array of art supplies. He prefers to invent his own way of doing things rather than to follow a preset procedure.

TIP: Encourage him to illustrate his meditations. Offer him blank paper, paints, and crayons. Avoid projects that do not allow for complete originality. For example, giving this child a blank piece of paper will offer more possibilities than offering him a picture to color. Also, work with him to create his own meditations.

~ A *high energy* child needs space to run and make loud noises. He also needs guidance to learn how to take the time to close his eyes and create a quiet adventure in his mind. The possibility of this kind of imaginative play may not ever have occurred to him, and if he tries it, he will discover how much fun the experience can be.

TIP: If your child is energetic, provide open areas for him to run around in, even during meditation time. Make games and toys available that encourage physical exercise. And teach quick-and-easy meditation techniques.

~ Similar to the creative child is the young person who *does not easily conform* to the standard mode of operation, and prefers instead to live his life in a unique way. Nonconforming behaviors can be interpreted as lack of attention; but have you noticed that children who show little concern for structure focus well on what interests them? Children who do not conform to rules can make teaching and parenting challenging, but many of the fearless leaders who have brought important change to our society did not easily conform as children. This quality allowed these individuals to break away from the norm and introduce new ways of thinking and being. Thomas Edison thought electricity might be a new way for the world to see. As a child, he was taken out of public school because he wouldn't stay focused. His mother homeschooled him, and later this nonconforming boy invented the incandescent light bulb.[1] Albert Einstein was deemed incompetent in math, but he went on to define the very essence of existence in ways that have physicists marveling to this day. Your little nonconformist may not change the way we see the world or invent something beneficial to mankind, but who knows what positive contribution his free-thinking might give to us all? In the short term, your recognition of his need to be his own unique version of a child, coupled with his very own meditation practice, will deepen his understanding of who he is and who he can be.

TIP: First and foremost, realize that you do not need your child's undivided attention—you can be a fantastic meditation guide without it. Children can benefit from an activity even if they do not appear to be paying attention. Allow your child to create and facilitate his own experience whenever possible. A child who loves Spiderman will be much more interested in meditations that involve his favorite movie characters than in some imagery you thought up on his behalf.

If you are working with several children, work in small groups and set fewer rules—remember that a low ratio of children to meditation guides makes it easier to facilitate experiences using fewer rules. Get to know each child personally and integrate each one's interests into your lesson, even if those interests seem an odd addition to your meditation exercises. (You might not understand the relevance of Spiderman, but a child could teach you volumes on the subject.) If one child's behavior is making it difficult for you and is affecting the experience of the rest of the group, be honest. Tell the child you are frustrated because his actions make it hard for you to work with the other children. You will be surprised at how many children will appreciate your honesty. They will respond more positively if you frame the situation in those terms than if you give them a set of rules.

~ A child who is *physically sensitive* might be allergic to certain foods, soaps, or fabrics. A child who is *emotionally sensitive* might be easily hurt by words.

TIP: Choose sensitive words when communicating with him, especially during meditation time. A sensitive child will associate any activity with emotional or physical discomfort if he is wounded while doing it. Also consider giving your child more whole foods, such as whole grains and fresh fruits and vegetables. What he eats before meditating will affect his meditation experience.

~ A child who is *intuitive* may tell you about his fantastic dreams or say exactly what you need to hear when you are down. The following list might help you notice an intuitive child.

- ❑ He is uniquely in tune with your emotional state.

- ❑ He knows how to behave in stressful situations.

- ❑ He is very good at sensing information about people he has just met.

❑ He remembers details from exciting dreams.

❑ He appears to hear or understand information from other realms of consciousness.

❑ He grasps new concepts quickly when they interest him.

❑ He is sensitive.

TIP: Listen intently to your child and honor all he shares with you. Encourage him to keep a dream journal. If he is young, he can keep a picture journal with drawings inspired by his dreams and meditations. Support his meditation experience by making it fun.

WORKING WITH CHILDREN WHO EXPRESS THEMSELVES QUIETLY, LOUDLY, WITH SADNESS, OR WITH DISINTEREST

The list of behaviors children exhibit is almost endless. Nevertheless, I include a few more below, not to define your child but to offer more examples of how he might experience his world, especially his new meditation practice.

~ **When a child is *quiet*, he might have much to say but feels timid about opening up, or he might prefer just to listen.**

TIP: Before and after meditation, let him know you are interested in what he is thinking and appreciate what he shares, but give him space and time to express himself when he is ready.

~ **A *loud* or *talkative* child expresses himself vocally. There may be a number of reasons why he has chosen this method, and as his meditation guide, you need to honor his need to express himself.**

TIP: Your child might use words to process his way through emotion. He might experience emotions in his body—tight muscles or a jittery feeling, for example—and need to let go of those uncomfortable feelings through speech. In this case, you can teach your child other methods of releasing physical and emotional feelings. The "Grounding Cord" in Chapter 8 is an excellent release meditation. You can also designate a special shouting time before or after meditation when you and your child yell at the top of your lungs. This activity is also great for quiet children, offering them a chance to explore their voices. It works especially well in groups, where all the shouts blend in together. These methods are not done to *hush* the child; instead, they offer him additional ways to express his feelings.

~ A child who is *unhappy* may be dealing with a self-esteem issue. Like the quiet child, this child needs special attention and blossoms when you convince him you are truly interested in what he has to share.

TIP: Make eye contact with your child, but allow him space to process his emotions. Be sensitive when finding out why he is sad, and trust yourself to offer the kind of assistance he needs. Lead him through meditations like "The Happy Tree," which will help him process sadness.

~ A child who is very *bright* may also be very *bored*. This child might not pay attention, and for good reason. He might know he will not benefit from the activity because he already understands the concept you are teaching.

TIP: Offer your child an extra challenge: ask him to create his own meditation, or help you facilitate an activity. Give him space to make suggestions for meditations and for activities afterward.

Whether you view your child as quiet, talkative, happy, or bored, take a moment before meditation to see him in a new light. Imagine that you have just met him for the first time. How does he shine his light to the world? Think about the infinite pool of feelings, sounds, sights, and smells your child senses, and how he processes them. What are some of the possible ways he might express himself in response to the stimuli in his environment and his inner world? Taking this time can be enlightening and humbling, as you see your child's complexity and beauty and as you understand how important it is that you, as a parent and meditation guide, see him as he truly is.

EFFECTIVE CLASSES FOR TEENS

Although many teens are more than willing to participate in discussions about meditation, generally speaking, one of the biggest differences between teaching young children how to meditate and teaching teens is that teenagers are more reluctant to speak up about their experiences. Therefore, do what you can to make teens feel comfortable. This includes not forcing them to speak or participate in every activity.

Working in small groups is one way to create a safe space for teens. Other suggestions include having teens text you or write down on a piece of paper anonymous questions that you can answer when you meet as a group. Stories about their meditation experiences can be gathered and shared in the same way.

Practicality is also important when working with teens. To connect what you are teaching to their daily lives, use real-life examples that students can relate to. You can rely on your own students to help you come up with real-life situations. For example, you might say to teens: "I am going to talk about the idea of surrender today. I use the word *surrender*, but if you were talking with your friends about this idea of letting go, you might not use this word. What word might you use, and what things might you want to let go of?"

The teens might come up with a variety of examples, including, "When someone doesn't want to go out with me anymore, I have to *stop* thinking about that person or I will go crazy." Or, "When I get grounded, I get so frustrated about staying home, so I just have to *accept* that I can't go anywhere." *Stop* and *accept* might be better terms to use when talking about surrender if your teens respond in this way.

Fun and creativity are not lost on teens even though they may be older than your other students. For example, guide teens to make handmade beads out of polymer clay. Then string the beads and ask your students to pull one bead over each time they repeat a mantra during meditation. This will help them keep track of how many mantras they have repeated. Or, have teens write down whatever they want to let go of on a small piece of paper. Then lead a ceremony during which each teen sets his or her paper into a fire.

GUIDING PRESCHOOLERS

When we work with preschoolers, teach each concept from the foundation and do not assume a child has previous understandings. For example, we might ask a preschooler to repeat a word silently in his head. However, the child might not know how to do this. I suggest first leading him to speak a word or sentence out loud. Then ask him to speak the word or sentence in a whisper. And finally, ask him to speak it silently. As an alternative to a single word or sentence, lead the child to count to ten aloud, in a whisper, and then silently.

Incorporating animals into lessons is also key, as preschoolers relate well to their furry little friends and adventurous reptiles. For instance, instead of asking a child to simply *sit still*, ask her to *sit still like a sleeping turtle*. Animals can also help us teach mindfulness. Ask your preschooler to imagine that she is a cat waiting for a mouse to come out of a hole in the wall. Tell her she must be very quiet, so the mouse does not know that she is watching. Then tell her she must watch without thinking about anything else; otherwise, the mouse could sneak out and run away while she is distracted.

This adventure can be played out entirely in her imagination with her eyes closed. Or, you can make the scenario into a game: One child plays the mouse hiding in a hole, perhaps under a chair covered with a blanket, while another child pretends that she is a cat waiting for the mouse. This is a fun way to help preschoolers develop concentration and mindfulness.

TEACHING GROUPS OF CHILDREN

Minutes before beginning a group class, consider challenging situations that the children may have recently faced. Perhaps one child has been forced to come to class; another might be sleeping from a sleepover the night before; yet another may have had an argument with a sibling, parent, or friend. Some children might even be hungry, have preconceived notions that meditation is stupid, or be nervous about doing something they've never done before.

If your students are not your child's classmates or playmates, some might be scared about being around kids they have never met. Use your imagination to prepare yourself for all the possibilities; use your sensitivity and intuition to accommodate all these children. Also, be sure to facilitate activities that adress all three learning styles. as discussed in Chapter 3.

CHILDREN WITH SPECIFIC CONDITIONS

If you know you will be working with a child with a certain diagnosis, familiarize yourself with the condition before the session. Conditions could include autism, Asperger's syndrome, and Tourette's syndrome. (Autism and Asperger's are discussed in detail in Chapter 7.) You may encounter children who have physical disabilities or Down syndrome; some may have intense anxiety, or they may have suffered from abuse, which has affected their emotional health. Do not be intimidated. Welcome each child and each situation, and know that you are capable of facilitating each child's meditation. Ask parents to accompany their children and participate if they feel comfortable. Be flexible in your approach: meditations might need to be shortened or simplified. Regardless of their physical health, condition, and background, all your students have the potential to benefit from meditation—and all will teach you, as well.

AVOIDING LABELS

After learning about creative, intuitive, quiet, and other types of children, being told not to use labels might seem contradictory. We help children when we understand their behaviors and use our knowledge to create the best learning environments possible. However, we can do this without taking that final step and labeling children. For example, we can learn about ADHD, make changes based on what we learn, yet not label the child. This subtle shift in perspective can be monumentous.

When we use labels to restrict our understanding of a child, we are apt to fulfill preconceived notions of who we think he is. This can inhibit the child's growth and force him into narrow behaviors. When, on the other hand, we remain open to the probability of our child behaving in ways outside of the label, we give him freedom to truly discover himself. Next time you use a label during your meditation time together, ask yourself: Is this label benefiting my child? Consider letting go of the label and welcoming new experiences for your child.

To better understand how labels affect people, take a moment to consider how you an others have labeled you in the past. Close your eyes and meditate on this. Pick a label you or others have placed on you. Does it feel good to attach this concept to your being or would it feel better to remove the label all together? Guiding yourself through this short exercise can open doors to deep understanding about how labels, even the positive ones, make us feel as if we are stuck in a box.

chapter 7

HELPING CHILDREN WITH ASPERGER'S AND AUTISM

A FIVE-YEAR-OLD BOY WITH AUTISM, named Tom, once participated in my meditation class. He sat in his mother's lap, to the right of me, and swayed his body back and forth during my instruction. Tom's eyes darted from the windows to the lights and then to the floor. His gaze never caught mine, which instinctually led me to believe that his attention never landed on what I was teaching.

I was very wrong. I posed a somewhat difficult question to the group of children. Answering this question required a keen observer. To my surprise, Tom promptly shared an excellent answer.

WHAT IS AUTISM AND ASPERGER'S?

A child diagnosed with *autism* has difficulty communicating and functioning in social situations. In addition, this child often fixates on one particular interest or activity. He is also likely to repeat behaviors and body movements, which can cause physical difficulties such as strained muscles and poor coordination. Another term, *Asperger's syndrome*, is simply high-functioning autism. Children diagnosed with Asperger's still suffer physically and navigate social satiations with difficultly, but not with as much struggle as children with severe autism.

HOW STRESS REDUCTION HELPS

Whether a child is diagnosed with autism or Asperger's, her social challenges cause anxiety. In addition, if the child is taken out of her daily routine or is required to focus on a subject other than the *special topic* she naturally and consistently gravitates to, unease will often set in.

Over the years, students have asked me if meditation helps children overcome symptoms of autism. Shelley Mannell, a physical therapist who teaches meditation to her young autistic clients, says stress-reduction techniques often help children with autism lead happier and more functional lives.

PREPARING FOR MEDITATION

Autistic children may flap their hands up and down or twist their entire body from side to side. Because Shelley ultimately wants to teach her young clients how to meditate, she first leads the children through yoga poses to settle down their bodies and *down-regulate* certain brain functions.

Flexed postures, such as child pose, can help a child become more relaxed. Downward-facing dog is also ideal because it offers resistance, since the child is pushing her own hands down into the floor. In addition to the yoga poses, Shelley pushes her hands into the child's hands to form a bridge and create resistance. These movements are beneficial because they provide the sensory input the child needs to calm her nervous system. This allows the child to better focus on the activity at hand.

Creating purpose: Children who are autistic are often hypersensitive to certain aspects of their environments. For example, you or I might not be distracted by the sound of a person munching peanuts; however, someone who is autistic might be so bothered by the crunching that to her the munching compares to a fleet of jets flying overhead. As a result, the child cannot focus on what she is working on or stay relaxed.

When Shelley begins meditation with a child, she affirms to the child, "Simply being in the world can be stressful, can't it?" Next, Shelley talks to the child about the benefits of meditation, especially how meditation can help the child feel more relaxed during situations that typically make her worried. (Shelley facilitates this discussion with high-functioning clients only.)

Shelley explains to the child that meditation calms us and softens anxiety-causing events so we can better attend to what is important. Meditation literally calms the child's brain, which is highly effective for children with autism.

Do not require children to close their eyes: Children with autism are generally afraid of letting go of their consciousness and, therefore, have difficulty going to sleep. A child with autism often associates closing her eyes with going to sleep. Therefore, she should not be asked to close her eyes during meditation because she might associate closing her eyes with fears about going to sleep.

Instead, invite the child to find a place where she is comfortable and able to listen. The child can lie down, sit, or stand. Shelley's young clients often sit in a bean-bag chair. Because the child's eyes are not closed, dim all lights and remove brightly colored wall hangings. Cover electronics and bookshelves with a plain sheet. And, turn off as many electronics as possible.

Furthermore, do not require children with autism to look at you. This request can cause additional stress. Autistic children are often in tune with what we say, whether they are looking at us or not. This is often true with non-autistic children as well.

INCORPORATING THE SENSES

Shelley often guides high-functioning clients through the Grounding Cord meditation described in Chapter 8. In addition, she also facilitates a waterfall guided-imagery experience with high-functioning clients. When working with children with lower-functioning autism, Shelley keeps meditations short and centers the experiences around each child's special interest.

Regardless of where the child falls on the autistic spectrum, incorporate as many senses as possible. For example, during the waterfall meditation, Shelley leads the child to visualize placing her hands underneath the falling water and to feel the temperature of the water. She also asks the child to see the water change color, eventually moving through each chakra color (chakras are discussed in Chapter 9). During another meditation, Shelley leads the child to imagine taking a bite of a cool, crisp, sweet apple. These details help the child shift her attention away from the annoyance of a clock ticking or the scratchy sensation of her shirt, and brings her attention inward.

CREATING MEDITATIONS FOR INDIVIDUAL CHILDREN

Creating a meditation from scratch might sound like a hefty task; however, it does not need to be. (See Chapter 12 for complete instructions on how to create a meditation for a child.) Because autistic children are typically preoccupied with a single television program, toy, or game, creating a meditation pivoting around the child's interest is paramount; not doing so will cause anxiety in most cases.

> Please note: Although Chapter 12 instructs the reader to interview the child, when working with autistic children, please avoid asking lots of questions. Fill in the blanks yourself based on your child's interests and simplify the story as much as possible by limiting the number of metaphors.

If the child is captivated with "Thomas the Tank Engine," the following brief journey meditation is appropriate:

See Thomas. Imagine he is covered in brown, sticky mud. Watch Thomas drive into the washing station. Hear the water shooting out of the hose onto Thomas. Smell the soapy water. Watch all of the dirt slide off Thomas. Now he is shinny and very happy. Gordon is smiling at Thomas. See how happy Thomas feels. Can you feel Thomas feeling happy and relaxed?

This meditation will help the child build her ability to calm her body and mind. Shelley often notices the child's face become more relaxed and her body turn less tense after such a meditation. What's more, the child can use this calming technique at another time.

Art Activity: Children with autism also benefit from following up meditations with an art activity. These projects should incorporate the child's interest and be geared towards her level of function. Moreover, be sensitive to any sensory challenges the child may have. For example, some autistic children become anxious when they touch wet or sticky substances; therefore, do not introduce paint or glue to these children.

SUPPORT FOR PARENTS

Shelley encourages families to continue meditation at home. In many cases, meditation becomes one of the most successful calming strategies for children with autism. Parents tell Shelley that their children are falling asleep more easily since they have been meditating, and that their children are less anxious. Shelley sends parents home with pre-recorded meditations. She also suggests that parents purchase additional meditation CDs and enroll their children in yoga classes.

Children with autism gain the most from a meditation practice when a good match is made between technique and child. For this reason, have a few ideas on hand and go with the flow—fitting advice for teaching meditation to any child.

chapter 8

Mindfulness and Other Centering Meditations

OUR STREAM OF CONSCIOUSNESS is simply a flowing series of thoughts running through our minds. Many people's stream of consciousness takes the form of an *internal monologue.* Consider what form your stream of consciousness takes. Do you think in pictures or words? Do you think in more than one voice? What influences your thoughts? You might find the answers to these questions intriguing.

Consider what thoughts sprout in your mind during a typical day. We think about a multitude of things, yet, you might be surprised how little time we actually devote to thinking about what we are doing in the present moment. We do not decide to think most of our thoughts; they simply develop in our minds unconsciously. Many of us spend endless hours mind-wandering, with little attempt to stop.

Do children experience their stream of consciousness in this way? In 1993, researchers at Stanford University brought children (one child at a time) into a room.[1] One researcher asked an assistant to sit and wait on the other side of the room facing a blank wall. Then the researcher asked the child if the assistant in the chair "is having some thoughts and ideas or is her mind empty of thoughts and ideas?" Ninety-five percent of the three-year-olds responded that the researcher's mind was empty of thoughts and ideas. Eighty percent of four-year-olds responded in this same way and forty-five percent of six- and seven-year-olds answered that the researcher's mind was empty of thoughts and ideas. In comparison five percent of adults answered as these children did when they were brought through the same process.

Chapter 5 covers the brain wave states of children. Two- to six-year-olds naturally experience a calm meditative state (called *Theta*).[2] Seven- to eleven-year-olds experience a quiet, yet open state (called *Alpha*). On the other hand, adults experience an analytical state (called *Beta*). Based on this, one could conclude that many children really do have naturally quiet, empty minds, a state many adults try hard to attain through meditation and other practices.

Controversy exists around teaching meditation to children, for a variety of reasons, one being that some people believe children are already in a meditative state. Although this might be true, concentration might not be a strong aspect of their ongoing meditative state. The meditations in this book promote concentration, and the meditations in this chapter are geared toward improving concentration and creating calm.

MINDFULNESS

Mindfulness is one of the most popular ways to help us improve concentration and settle our minds. When we practice mindfulness the result can be compared to a jar filled with water and sand. When the jar is shaken, the grains of sand whirl around in somewhat arbitrary directions. However, if we set the jar down, we can watch the sand settle to the bottom, leaving the water clear. This clear water represents a still mind. When we teach children to how to notice their environments, thoughts, and feelings, we help them still their minds and improve their focus. These results yield many benefits, including better attentiveness, more contentment, and improved relationships.

Mindfulness and concentration help us come to center. Children can find their center by practicing breathing exercises. Or they can repeat a mantra to help them calm their bodies and minds. Children can also use progressive relaxation, commonly used by hypnotherapists to educe a deep state of relaxation, to find their center. This practice involves relaxing each muscle group one at a time, beginning with the feet and ending with the facial muscles.

This chapter offers five centering meditations. The first is a mindfulness exercise. The second is a simple breathing activity. The third uses a mantra. The fourth offers grounding and the last will help your child drift off to sleep.

~MINDFULNESS MEDITATION~

Ask your child to sit or lie down comfortably with his eyes closed. Then lead him through this mini-meditation, during which he will have the opportunity to use all five of his outer senses to truly experience the present moment. He can answer the questions aloud or silently to himself.

Take in a deep breath. Feel your body resting on the floor or chair. Does the floor or chair feel soft or hard? Feel your clothes resting on your body. Do they feel scratchy or smooth? See if you can feel your heartbeat. *(Pause.)* Now listen to what is going on around you. Can you hear any sounds? If not listen to the silence. *(Pause.)* With your eyes closed, look at the back of your eyelids. What does this look like? *(Pause, then spray a fragrance in the air.)* Take in a deep breath. Do you smell anything? What does it smell like? *(Hand your child a bite-sized piece of yummy fruit.)* Put this fruit in your mouth and chew it slowly. What does is taste like? Tangy? Sweet? Sour? Enjoy this taste as long as you like.

After Meditation Questions:

1. What did you feel?
2. What did the back of your eyelids look like?

3. What did you smell?
4. What did you taste?

BELLY BREATHING

When my daughter finishes her dinner, she loves to get out of her seat and tries to persuade me to play with her. When this happens, I help her find something to do while I finish my meal and my conversation with my husband. Similarly, one of the best ways I use to quiet my mind is to give it something to concentrate on. Giving the mind something to focus on helps my consciousness forget the need for excitement and drama and helps it just *be*.

I might ask my consciousness to focus on a vision of a leaf, an imaginary soothing bell tone, or my breath. Or I might choose something more arbitrary, like my right thumb or a physical sensation in my body, such as a cramp in my jaw or a cool sensation on my arm. I call each of these a *point of focus*.

Do I stay centered on my point of focus throughout meditation? Absolutely not. My mind wanders into thoughts about the point of focus—and much more! For example, while focusing on an image of a leaf, I might be reminded of a trip to Colorado and the friends there and things we did together, then I'll think of the color of the mountains, and that will remind me of a dream I had last night . . . When I notice I have lost concentration, I simply return my attention back to the point of focus. I don't judge myself for losing attention, I just bring my focus back. With practice I am able to catch myself more often and return to the point of focus more easily.

In Zen meditation, a form of Buddhist practice, the meditator focuses on the breath. When thoughts arise, the meditator does not pay attention to them, but lets them go. This method—to acknowledge thoughts and not cling to them—allows you to recognize that thoughts in themselves really have no power. They arise and then they disappear. This form of meditation is effective in bringing peace to the mind and body, as you focus on simply breathing.

Many of the meditations in this book are adventures that will entertain your child, but the following mindfulness meditation encourages him to rest in a still place in his mind and to gently let go of his thoughts. If done properly, this meditation will yield the same results as the "Grounding Cord" meditation, leaving the child feeling calm, focused, and centered.

~ME AND MY ZEN MEDITATION~

If your child is quite young, before the meditation ask him to lay down with a small stuffed animal resting on his belly. Beanie Babies work best because they lay flat on moving bellies and have eyes that patiently gaze back at children. Since this meditation focuses on breathing, you might also consider putting a dab of sweet smelling essential oil on your child's wrist so he can smell it during meditation. Then read the following instructions to your child.

Take in a deep breath, and then let it out. Take in another deep breath, and look at your stuffed animal resting on your belly. Let's do this five times with your eyes open, looking at your belly: One, breathe . . . Two, breathe . . . Three, breathe . . . Four, breathe . . . Five, breathe.

Close your eyes now and keep breathing in and out, but this time, without opening your eyes, imagine that the stuffed animal is rising and falling on your belly. If you'd like, count your breaths. While you do this, you might notice yourself thinking about something else besides the stuffed animal rising and falling on your belly. If you do notice a thought, say to yourself, "Oh, I'm thinking about my video game right now (*or whatever he might be thinking about*). Now I'm going to think about my breathing, my belly, and my stuffed animal again."

I'm going to give you some time to do this on your own. If you need to take a peek at your belly while you're breathing to remember what it looks like, go right ahead. Then close your eyes again. (*Pause for 15 to 30 seconds.*)

Open your eyes whenever you are finished.

After Meditation Questions:

1. What was your favorite part of the meditation?
2. Did you notice thoughts about other things besides your breathing?
3. Did you feel anything in your body, or have an emotional feeling during your meditation?
4. How do you feel now?

This meditation is easily modified for older children who might balk at a Beanie Baby. They can peek at their belly sans Beanie Baby, watching it rise and fall. The object is to have something the child can return his focus to, as thoughts arise and pass through his mind. Adult Zen meditators focus on the *hara*, a point about two inches below the naval, which scientists refer to as the bottom of the solar plexus, a network of nerves. The meditator simply returns his focus to his breathing and the *hara* as thoughts arise. Some older children are quite capable of this technique, as well.

CHANTING

A mantra is a word or phrase that is repeated silently as a point of focus during meditation. Traditionally, mantras are words that do not invoke thought, but instead help create a rhythmic flow of breath and serenity. Many mantras are composed of Sanskrit syllables. Sanskrit is the ancient language in which many Hindu scriptures are written. In the Hindu tradition, students are given life-long mantras by their gurus and are told to never share them with anyone. Over 30 years ago, my grandfather took a course in Transcendental Meditation where he received a secret mantra. Still, after all these years, I have yet to convince him to share it with me.

If your child is old enough to read, then write several personalized mantras on separate pieces of paper. Place all the mantras in a bowl. Before your mantra meditation, offer the bowl to the child so he can pick out his mantra for the day. He can either keep it as a secret or tell the world. Keeping secret mantras can be fun, but it isn't necessary.

Here are some Sanskrit mantras with their English translations. Use either the Sanskrit word or the English word, or create your own.

Om—Sound of the universe

Shanti—Peace

These can be said separately or together. Together: *Om shanti shanti shanti*

Mani—Jewel *(ma-nee)*

Padme—Lotus *(pawd-may)*

Together: *Om Mani Padme Hum:* I bring compassion and wisdom.

Below are mantras without translation, if you feel you would be distracted by knowing their meaning.

Sat Nam (soft *a's*)

Sita Ram

Jai Ma

~ME AND MY MANTRA MEDITATION~

Close your eyes. Take in a deep breath. Then breathe it back out with a sigh. Now when you breath in, imagine your breath going down into your lungs. When you breath out, imagine it going back out of your lungs and out of your mouth. Another deep breath in, and let it out with a big sigh. Now take a breath in, and as you breathe out say your mantra silently to yourself.

(Breathe aloud one full inhalation and exhalation.)

Breathe in again, and say your mantra as you breathe out. Continue to breath and hear your mantra in your mind. If you like, make your mantra softer and softer, then louder and louder. If you forget to say your mantra, that's okay, just say it again when you remember.

(Continue to breathe aloud so your child can hear you. Frequently remind him to say his mantra as he breathes out. Continue the meditation as long as it feels appropriate. If your child is under 10 years old, or is doing this meditation for the first time, end the meditation after three or four minutes.)

After Meditation Questions
1. What happened when you followed your breath in and out of your lungs?
2. Was it easy to remember to say your mantra?
3. What other thoughts came into your mind in between mantras?
4. Do you like your mantra?

Variations
If it is more comfortable, have your child say his mantra as he breathes in instead of on the exhale. Or he can say it during both the inhale and exhale. The idea is for him to feel the rhythm of his breathing and the mantra together.

Instead of the mantra, you can use an alternate point of focus like an imaginary flower or animal, or a feeling like warmth or happiness. And lastly, a single sound can replace the mantra, like a bell ringing or running water. These sounds can be real or imagined. When your child uses his imagination to hear the bell or running water, or to see a flower in his mind, he will develop his inner senses of sight, feeling, and hearing.

Saying the mantra aloud is another variation. This is called chanting, which is also a wonderful way for children to find focus.

Progressive Relaxation

Our brains create energy in the form of electromagnetic waves, or brain waves. These waves can be measured by an instrument called an electroencephalograph (EEG), which detects the four primary wave patterns: beta (averaging 21 cycles per second), alpha (about 10 cycles per second), theta (about 6 cycles per second), and delta (about 4 cycles per second). During sleep we experience theta and delta waves as well as during meditation. Someone who has difficulty falling asleep usually has a hard time slowing his brain waves from beta to alpha. Once he is in an alpha state, he can usually slip into theta, and then deeper into a delta sleeping state.[3]

We can enter the alpha state by clearing our minds of daily thoughts, and focusing instead on peaceful images, sounds, or mantras; or we can use our breath or progressive relaxation techniques to shift our minds into other states of consciousness. The following journey meditation uses breath and progressive relaxation. This simple meditation will help your child move his consciousness from beta to alpha, and eventually into a theta/delta sleep state.

~ Sleepy Cloud Meditation~

Before the meditation, talk to your child about his bedtime routine. What does he usually do before bed? Have him describe any and all aspects of his routine, such as brushing his teeth and being tucked into bed. Then read the following meditation to your child.

Part 1
Close your eyes. You can put your hands over your eyes if you want to. (*Briefly talk with your child about his bedtime*

routines.) Now imagine that you are ready for bed. See yourself getting into your bed.

Part 2

Keep your eyes closed and take in a deep breath. Now when you breathe back out, feel your body relaxing. We are going to do this four more times. Take a deep in-breath, and then relax your legs when you breathe out. Take another deep in-breath, and this time relax your arms as you breathe out. Deep breath in again, and relax your shoulders and neck as you breathe out. Deep breath in, and feel your body relax more. Take one more deep breath in, and as you breathe out, feel how sleepy your body is.

Now see yourself lying in bed, relaxed and sleepy. See a soft, sleepy cloud floating above your head. This cloud can be any color you want, but remember it is a *sleepy* cloud. You might even hear the cloud playing soft music. As this cloud gets close to your face, feel your eyes get sleepy. They itch a little and are very heavy and tired. They might even water a little bit. Now feel yourself falling asleep. I will give you a moment to see yourself sleeping. (*Pause, then repeat Part 2 until the child is asleep.*)

This meditation is meant to be done in bed while the child is going to sleep. Feel free to add any steps specific to your child. After practicing the meditation for several weeks, add more muscle groups for your child to relax, such as the belly, head, and feet. Explain to your child that if he is not asleep at the end of Part 2, you will repeat the steps.

If your child experiences fear, such as fear of the dark, lead him through "The Happy Tree" meditation in Chapter 11, changing the *sad* fruit to *scared* fruit. This meditation will help you and your child discover what he needs to find comfort.

GROUNDING

Have you ever been nervous before a speaking engagement, irritable after a sleepless night, or felt nauseous or hot after an argument? If so, you probably were not grounded. As discussed in Chapter 1, grounding meditations bring calmness and focus, as they bring us into balance with the natural rhythms of the earth. When we are ungrounded, we become nervous, easily irritable, or even nauseous.

We live in a world mostly defined by opposites, such as *holding on* and *letting go*. As grounded as we may become, we must also be as willing to let go. It is in both holding and releasing that we ease through change. Letting go of what keeps us from being grounded doesn't mean that what we're letting go of is bad. It just means that we do not want or need to hold on to it at this time.

When we observe our minds, bodies, and spirits letting go of feelings, images, and sounds in meditation, we release *energy*. In other words, we experience the essence being released through our senses. We might *see* energies move out of our body as if we were watching a movie, or we might *feel* a sense of release, physically or emotionally. At other times, we might *hear* energy escape. When your child is ungrounded, he may experience voices, images, and emotions bouncing around in his head. He can relax himself by letting go of these feelings, memories, and thoughts during the following journey meditation.

~GROUNDING CORD MEDITATION~

Close your eyes. You can put your hands over your eyes if you want to. Now take a deep in-breath. When you breathe back out, feel your body relaxing. We'll take two more breaths. Deep breath in, and relax your legs as you breathe out. Deep breath in, and relax your arms and neck as you breathe out.

Imagine a cord connected to your root chakra at the bottom of your tailbone. Then see this cord go down into the floor. This cord can look or feel like anything you choose. See this cord go down through the floor, into the ground underneath this building. See the cord continue through the ground all the way to the center of the planet. Feel this cord connect to the center of the planet. Now feel yourself attached to the center of the planet by your cord. Once you feel this connection, imagine particles of energy moving down from your head to your root chakra (at the bottom of your tailbone) and down the cord. You might see this energy as particles, or you might see pictures coming out of your head and going down the cord. If you see something in particular go down the cord, that does not mean it is bad. It's just a thought that you don't need right now, energy you don't need and are sending to the center of the earth.

See this energy drop all the way to the center of the planet. You might even hear the energy go down the cord. What does it sound like? Now see energy come from your hands and arms down through your stomach and down your cord. It travels to the center of the planet because you don't need it anymore. Now feel this energy move out from all the areas in your body. Listen to the energy move from your chest down to the center of the planet. See this energy come from your feet and legs and go down your grounding cord.

I'll give you a few moments to do this on your own. Let

any unneeded energy fall down the cord. Notice how clear and clean you feel. *(Pause.)*

Now thank yourself for all the things you released. *(Pause.)* You can open your eyes whenever you are ready.

After Meditation Questions

1. What did your cord look like?
2. What did you see go down your cord? Did you hear it?
3. Did you feel anything in your body while you did this?
4. Do you feel different?
5. Do you think you could do this meditation on your own?

A NOTE OF CAUTION

Some psychologists claim that meditation has not been proven safe for children's developing brains. Some Hindu teachers caution not to teach meditation to children under eight years old. These warnings are in regard to meditations involving focused concentration on a single element. In this book, "Me and My Zen" and "Me and My Mantra" are the only meditations that fall into this category. As long as children are enjoying the process, use these meditations. Otherwise, stick to meditations that offer more of a story and a journey to help them develop concentration. The reason being, we do not want to turn off children to the idea of meditating.

I recommend you do not use "Me and My Zen" and "Me and My Mantra" meditations more than a few minutes a day with your younger children. If children 12 and older wish to use them for longer periods of time, then support their decision.

And, never force your child to do any meditation, whether it be a mindfulness or a journey meditation. If children are forced to meditate, they are less likely to meditate as adults. And even more importantly, the negative experience might cause trauma, which could affect other aspects of their lives.

MORE FUN BEFORE AND AFTER THE MEDITATIONS

Let Go Hokey Pokey

This activity is just like the traditional "Hokey Pokey," but instead of putting our right foot (and other body parts) in and shaking it all about, a thought, emotion, or physical feeling is put into the circle. Before conducting this activity, you will need to talk about *release*. Tell your child that release means letting go of something, and that we can let go of all kinds of things. We can let go of feelings, fears, memories, and thoughts. As in the "Grounding Cord" meditation, be certain to reassure your child that whatever he wants to let go of is not necessarily bad—it's just something he does not want to hold on to right now.

Ask your child what kinds of things he could let go of. Explain that you will be doing the "Let Go Hokey Pokey," and encourage him to pick something he wants to let go of. You can start by placing your item in the circle first, while you lead your child through the song and gestures. When you place the thought, emotion, or physical feeling into the circle, place your hands in the circle as though you were holding on to it, and shake it. Then repeat the song, filling in the blanks with whatever your child chooses to let go of. This activity is especially fun with a group. And be sure to stand up so you can move freely.

> You put your _____ in,
> You take your _____ out;
> You put your _____ in,
> And you shake it all about.
> You do the Hokey-Pokey,
> And you turn yourself around.
> That's what it's all about!

Raisin Experiment

Give a child a raisin to hold. Then ask the child to put the raisin up to his nose. Ask him to describe what the raisin smells like. Next guide the child to set the raisin on his tongue. Ask him to describe the raisin's texture. Then ask the child to chew the fruit slowly and describe how it tastes. This is an excellent way to help children learn mindfulness.

What Is My Dream? Game

This game is fun before bedtime or any time of the day. Ask your child to act out a dream he had recently. Then guess what he is doing in his dream. This form of charades encourages him to use his imagination and allows him to deal with dream content at a close to conscious level. You can also ask questions about the elements of the dream that will help him understand his dream.

Art Projects

1. Have your child draw a picture of himself and his grounding cord.
2. Make physical representations of grounding cords out of yarn, string, or fabric. Cut pieces of yarn or other material at least three feet long. Have your child tie objects such as pictures, toys, cotton balls, or noodles to the cord, representing what he is letting go of. Attach the cords to the ceiling, or put them away until the next meditation.
3. If your child is old enough, have him write a poem about his meditation experience on a 9-by-12 inch piece of construction paper. Attach the poem to a piece of 12-by-18 inch construction paper. Have him decorate the construction paper that frames the poem.

These exercises and projects, and those in subsequent chapters, let children explore their meditation experiences. In doing them, your child not only creates an artistic representation of his experiences, he creates an opportunity to find meaning in meditation. Through questions about how he feels and thinks about his experiences, you can help him gain a deeper understanding of himself. These activities also help you understand your child better. As you do, you can choose future meditations more effectively. And, of course, these activities are fun. Associating meditation with fun will keep your child interested in inner exploration for a lifetime.

chapter 9

Healing My Body

Children are intrigued by their bodies as they witness themselves transform into an older, stronger, bigger person each year. This chapter shares a simple way to help your child talk to her body. It also describes the subtle energy around her body, the aura, and the seven chakras (or energy centers) located from the crown of the head to the bottom of her spine. Teaching your child how to have a good relationship with her body will help her stay healthy and strong.

Mind Body Connection

In the first chapter, I shared a personal story about a conversation I had with my body during meditation: my body informed me that prisoners stood behind bars located in my left brain, a metaphor for my thoughts. I became aware that if I allowed my thoughts and words to flow more freely, my tightened jaw would release itself. And it did. This showed me that when we listen to our inner promptings, we learn what our bodies need to be healthy. Sometimes what we hear and see are literal answers; at other times they are symbolic, as in my example. Children love to talk to and listen to their bodies, and meditation gives them the power to access what their bodies are telling them they need to be healthy.

Before guiding your child through the following meditation, place a stuffed animal in front of her and ask her to close her eyes. Then guide her to ask the stuffed animal a question, such as: What is your favorite color? What it your favorite food? How do you feel today? Afterward, give her an opportunity to share what she heard. This will help your child practice listening to her inner voice. Older children might prefer communicating with a plant during this warm-up exercise. However, I use stuffed animals with students of all ages.

~WHAT DOES MY BODY HAVE TO SAY? MEDITATION~

Close your eyes. You can put your hands over your eyes if you want to. Now take a deep in-breath. When you breathe back out, feel your body relaxing. We'll take two more breaths. Deep breath in, and relax your legs as you breathe out. Deep breath in, and relax your arms and neck as you breathe out.

Now it is time to listen to your body and find out what your body needs. Let's begin with your right foot. Go ahead and say hello to your right foot. You can do that with your eyes closed. "Hi, Foot." Now ask your foot what it needs. "Foot, what do you need today?" And listen for your answer. *(Pause.)* Is there anything you would like to tell your foot? Go ahead and tell this to your foot. Does your left foot have anything to tell you?

Let's talk to your tummy now. "Hi, Tummy." Now ask your tummy what it needs. "Tummy, what do you need today?" And listen for your answer. *(Pause.)* Is there anything you would like to tell your tummy? Go ahead and tell this to your tummy.

Let's talk to your heart now. "Hi, Heart." Ask your heart what it needs. "Heart, what do you need today?" And listen for your answer. *(Pause.)* Is there anything you would like to tell your heart? Go ahead and tell this to your heart.

Notice how you feel. Go ahead and open your eyes whenever you are ready.

Depending on the age of your child, you might continue with more body parts, or ask her what body part she would like to talk with next. Older children might like to ask their internal organs, spine, or other inner parts what they need. If your child is struggling with a particular physical issue, invite her to talk to that part of her body. After meditation, help your child do what she can to fulfill her body's needs.

After Meditation Questions
1. What did your foot, tummy, and heart tell you they needed?
2. Is there anything you want to give to your body?
3. If your child didn't *hear* anything, ask: Did you get a feeling from your body or did you see something when you asked the questions?

CHAKRA BALANCING

The fluid energy that moves through our chakras is *subtle energy*. Depending on the tradition and the language, subtle energy is also called life force energy, *Chi, Ki, Qi, mana* and *etheric energy*. Our subtle energy leaves our bodies when we die, which is why it is sometimes called *life-force energy*. This energy runs through our chakras and auras, and emits a vibration from our bodies. Scientists describe this energy as the low-intensity electromagnetic energy around and within our bodies, while metaphysicians explain subtle energy as the nonmaterial fabric of the universe.

The aura is not mentioned in these meditations, but it is also an important part of our subtle energetic system and worth mentioning. Subtle energy moves through the chakras and spills out of our bodies, forming an energy field around us. Auras and chakras are not physical, but they function in ways similar to the physical body.

Like skin, our auras surround us; and like organs, our chakras work together to circulate and clean the subtle energy that runs through our subtle bodies. (There is an activity to help your child feel her aura at the end of this chapter.)

Chakras pump energy through the subtle body, much like the heart pumps blood through veins. You can imagine the chakras as seven hearts pumping, but unlike the beating heart, the chakras spin. In fact, *chakra* is a Sanskrit word meaning *wheel*.

As is the case with the physical heart, it is vital that the chakras be clear and unobstructed. Meditation masters teach that our physical bodies suffer when our chakras are clogged. They teach us to cleanse our chakras by working through our emotions. We clean our chakras by meditating, doing yoga poses, participating in psychotherapy, or doing any other practice that heals us. Chakras are energy centers that help us maintain physical, emotional, mental, and spiritual balance. They are located throughout our *subtle body*. The subtle body is the framework of fluid energy that rests in and around the physical body. Children are particularly interested in their subtle bodies because these shift and change even more quickly than their physical bodies. Seven main chakras are located along the core meridian, from the bottom of the tailbone to the tip of the head. The Chakra Chart provided in this section shows the location of all seven main chakras. We also have hundreds of smaller chakras along other meridians throughout our bodies. Some of these smaller chakras are used as acupuncture points.

Chakras have varying frequencies—the higher the frequency, the healthier the chakra. Each one resonates with a specific musical note, or vibration, which is out of the range of human hearing. Each chakra also emits a particular color wave, whose frequency is higher than most of us can perceive. When we raise the frequency of our chakra energy, we raise the musical vibration to higher octaves and increase the vibrancy of the color wave.[1]

The chakras are intimately related to our bodily functions. Each has its corresponding gland in the endocrine system. For example, the thyroid gland is related to and influenced by the throat chakra, and the condition of the throat chakra affects the organs that rely on the thyroid gland. When the throat chakra is strengthened, the thyroid and other systems are positively affected.

As the Chakra Chart shows, each chakra helps us in a special way. These specific functions are based on yogic tradition dating back thousands of years.

There are many ways to strengthen our chakras, all of which can be done during meditation. We can listen to the musical note that corresponds to the chakra, we can visualize a brilliant color that corresponds to the chakra, or we can revisit an experience that took place when the particular chakra was strong. For example, since the job of our first chakra is to help us be strong and confident, thinking of a time when we felt confident strengthens the first chakra.

~ STRONG CHAKRAS MEDITATION ~

During this meditation, pause for about fifteen seconds between each chakra.

Close your eyes. You can put your hands over your eyes if you want to. Now take a deep in-breath. When you breathe back out, feel your body relaxing. We'll take two more breaths. Deep breath in, and relax your legs as you breathe out. Deep breath in, and relax your arms and neck as you breathe out.

Think about your first chakra. It is at the bottom of your tailbone, where your butt sits on the floor. Now remember a time when you felt very strong. *(Pause.)*

Now move your attention to your second chakra, where your belly button is. Think about one of your favorite feelings—maybe happiness, excitement, or a feeling of peacefulness. *(Pause.)*

Now move your attention to your third chakra, between your belly button and your heart. You can touch it with your hand if you want. Think of something that you really understand, like 4 + 4 = 8 or how to put a puzzle together. *(Pause.)*

Move your attention to your fourth chakra, your heart chakra, and think of someone you love very much. This person can be yourself. *(Pause.)*

Now move your attention to your fifth chakra, your throat chakra, and remember a time when you told somebody something that was really important to you. *(Pause.)*

Move your attention to your sixth chakra, between your eyes, and think about how easy it is to shut your eyes and see pictures with your imagination. Or look at a person, a pet, or a place in your mind. *(Pause.)*

Move your attention to your seventh chakra, at the top of your head, and imagine that everything around you loves you. The trees love you. The furniture loves you. All the people in the room love you. The floor loves you. *(Pause.)*

Notice how you feel. Go ahead and open your eyes whenever you are ready.

After Meditation Questions

1. How do you feel? Do you feel different?
2. Did you feel your chakras get stronger or bigger, or opening up?
3. What were some of the thoughts you used during the meditation

to open your chakras? When did you feel strong and confident?
4. What did you see or hear during your meditation?

~CLEAN CHAKRAS MEDITATION~

Close your eyes. You can put your hands over your eyes if you want to. Now take a deep in-breath. When you breathe back out, feel your body relaxing. We'll take two more breaths. Deep breath in, and relax your legs as you breathe out. Deep breath in, and relax your arms and neck as you breathe out.

Imagine a colored ball of energy above your head. Fill this ball of energy with smiles, hugs, and some of your favorite feelings, people, and things. *(Pause.)* Now see the energy from this ball coming through the top of your head, through your crown chakra. Feel this energy clean out anything heavy or dark in this chakra. Watch any heavy or dark energies naturally fall down to your root chakra and out through a grounding cord into the center of the planet. Now see more energy come into your crown chakra at the top of your head and move through your brow chakra, which is between your eyes. Feel this energy clean out your brow chakra. If you want, you can ask an animal to help you clean out your chakras. *(Pause.)*

See more energy come into the top of your head from the ball of energy above your head. Feel this energy pass through your crown and brow chakras all the way through your throat chakra. What does it sound like? Feel the energy clean out your throat chakra. Remember, you can ask an animal to help you clean out your chakras. *(Pause.)*

Now feel even more energy come through your chakras from above, moving through the throat chakra to your heart chakra. Feel the energy clean out this chakra. Feel any heavy or dark energies fall down to your root chakra, where you sit on the floor. Then see this energy go down a grounding cord to the center of the planet. *(Pause.)* Be aware of more energy coming through your chakras from above your head to your solar plexus chakra, which is below your heart and above your belly button. Feel the energy moving through this chakra, cleaning it out. *(Pause.)* Then see the energy continuing to your belly button chakra. Feel any dark or heavy energy falling to the center of the planet through your grounding cord. Listen to it fall to the center of the planet. *(Pause.)*

Now see the flow of energy through all your chakras including the root chakra, which is at the bottom of your tailbone where you sit on the floor. *(Pause.)* Feel this flow of energy move from the top of your head to the bottom of your tailbone, and down your grounding cord into the center of the planet.

You can open your eyes whenever you are ready.

After Meditation Questions

1. How do you feel? Do you feel different?
2. What color was the energy flowing through your chakras?
3. What did the heavy and dark energy look or sound like?
4. Did you feel your chakras get stronger or bigger, or open up?

CHAKRA CHART

Number	Location	Color	Musical Note	Job
1	Root (tailbone)	Red	C (do)	Helps us be strong and confident.
2	Belly Button (navel)	Orange	D (re)	Helps us feel sad, happy, excited, etc.
3	Top of Belly (solar plexus)	Yellow	E (me)	Helps us think and understand. Helps us when we are confused.
4	Heart	Green	F (fa)	Helps us love other people and ourselves.
5	Throat	Blue	G (so)	Helps us talk (express ourselves) to other people.
6	Between the Eyes (brow)	Purple	A (la)	Helps us see images with our eyes closed. Helps us see into the future and into the past.
7	Top of the Head (crown)	White	B (ti)	Helps when we feel left out. Helps us feel included.

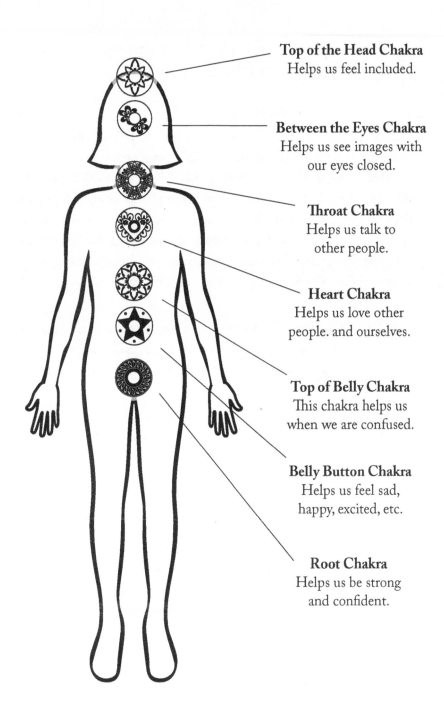

Top of the Head Chakra
Helps us feel included.

Between the Eyes Chakra
Helps us see images with
our eyes closed.

Throat Chakra
Helps us talk to
other people.

Heart Chakra
Helps us love other
people. and ourselves.

Top of Belly Chakra
This chakra helps us
when we are confused.

Belly Button Chakra
Helps us feel sad,
happy, excited, etc.

Root Chakra
Helps us be strong
and confident.

MORE FUN BEFORE AND AFTER THE MEDITATIONS

The following two exercises help children experience their subtle energy. It makes the abstract tangible.

Learning How to Feel Auras

Our auras are fields of subtle energy that surround our bodies. Although this energy is said to be invisible, people who are clairvoyant are able to see it. For those lacking this ability, scientists (especially those who study acupuncture) have created measuring devices to detect and record the fields generated by auras. These devices show that the location, color, and frequency of auras fluctuate. Sometimes they rest about a foot from the body, and other times they expand out to several feet. The following exercise can teach your child how to feel her aura.

1. Rub your hands together to stimulate the nerve endings and chakras in your hands, and ask your child to do the same. Mention that this makes her hands more sensitive to touching things, especially subtle energy.

2. Hold one of your hands a few inches from your chest with your palm facing toward your chest, and ask your child to do the same with her own hand over her own chest.

3. Slowly move your hand away from your chest, and notice where you feel a difference in energy. Ask your child to do the same. Explain that it is easier if she does this with her eyes closed, while moving her hand back and forth slightly as she moves it outward. All the motions should be slow. The aura might feel like a denser form of energy, like pushing on a balloon; or she might feel a change in temperature.

Have you ever noticed that sensing the aroma of someone else's house is easier than sensing the smells in your own home? We become desensitized to the smells in our own houses because we experience them every day and every night. Likewise, sometimes feeling another person's aura is easier than feeling your own because the frequency of the energy emanation differs from your own. You can repeat the above exercise, helping your child to feel *your* aura.

Learning How to Feel Chakras

Auras and chakras are made of the same energy, so feeling our chakras is similar to feeling our auras. Use the following steps to teach your child how to feel someone's chakras. When your child feels your chakras, she might feel heat, density (like the outside of a balloon), or some other sensation. It is good subtle energy etiquette to remember to ask permission before feeling another's aura or chakras, and to ask your child to do the same.

1. Ask your child to rub her hands together to stimulate the nerve endings and chakras in her hands.

2. Ask her to place her hand about four inches above *your* heart chakra. Ask her to move her hand around a bit until she feels the energy of your chakra.

3. Repeat with two other chakras.

4. Switch roles and repeat.

If you like, have your child hold a pendulum a few inches above each of your chakras while you lie down. See what happens.

Art Projects

1. Have your child draw a picture of herself running her energy through her chakras.

2. Cut a piece of butcher paper larger than your child. Have her lie down on the paper, and use a marker to draw an outline of her body. Your child can use paint, markers, or crayons to draw each chakra into her outlined body. Encourage her to add pictures of things she associates with each chakra.

Writing Activity

If your child is old enough, have her write down the steps of one of the meditations in her own words.

Modification for "Strong Chakras Meditation"

In the "Strengthening My Chakras" meditation in this chapter, you asked your child to remember past events and to experience love. In this version, ask her to sing the note that corresponds to each chakra. You might choose to use the musical scale: *do, re, mi, fa, so, la, ti, do.*

chapter 10

RENEWING SPIRIT

MEDITATION IS A WONDERFUL AVENUE TO DELIGHT. Meditation renews our spirit: with it, we feed ourselves a delicious dish of joy tossed with excitement and topped with a bit of laughter. All of the meditations in this book offer soul nourishment and spiritual renewal; however, this chapter offers three meditations that will nourish your child's spirit in specific ways. The first one will guide your child to bring his favorite feelings and energies into his being. The second will help him heal pain from past conflicts. The third is inspired by cotemplative practice.

SPIRITUAL NURISHMENT

Just as when we eat we refuel our energy, when we meditate we nourish our spirit. It is as easy as giving yourself a big, happy hug. Meditation is available anytime and anywhere as a means to refuel spiritual energy supplies and gain physical energy, too.

Every tradition recognizes and honors subtle, nurturing energy in its own way, and gives this energy various names. Native American traditions calls upon Father Sky and Mother Earth when referring to the earth's nurturing energy and that of the powerful, awe-inspiring sky. The Chinese refer to these same energies as yin and yang, yin being the feminine and yang being the masculine. Cultivating yin and yang within our being balances us, feeds us, and renews us.

The female and male essences exist inside and outside of each one of us, regardless of our gender. Over the past 30 years, women have moved toward reclaiming their male essence either by making their way into the workforce or by staying at home with their children and valuing this nurturing work as much as the role of the working father. Men, in turn, have accessed their female side by expressing emotions more easily and trusting their intuition. In some cases, a woman may already have a strong male essence and needs to nurture her feminine side to feel balanced, while another woman needs to unleash her male side. And the same goes for men. No matter how our male and female essences manifest, we need to honor and balance both within us.

While practicing the following meditation inspired by the Native American tradition, your child will pull from the earth and from the cosmos elements that nourish his soul. It is best if he imagines simple images and the feelings they elicit, such as a smile, laughter, warm sunlight, or a hug from a friend. No image is right or wrong; the only requirement is that it gives your child joy. This journey meditation will help him wake up happily in the morning, or lift his spirits any time during the day.

~FUDGE SWIRL MEDITATION~

Close your eyes. You can put your hands over your eyes if you want to. Now take a deep in-breath. When you breathe back out, feel your body relaxing. We'll take two more breaths. Deep breath in, and relax your legs as you breathe out. Deep breath in, and relax your arms and neck as you breathe out.

See a ball of light above your head. Fill this ball of light with some of your favorite things, maybe a smile, your favorite color, or your favorite toy or favorite food. You can even put laughter into your ball of light. As you bring more good things into your ball of light and energy, see the ball get larger and larger. Let the stars, the sun, and the moon help you bring good things into your ball of energy. You may even feel starlight or a sunbeam touch your ball of energy. See the ball of energy get even bigger. You can put pictures of your favorite places, favorite people, or favorite things into your ball of light. As you put these pictures into your ball of light, notice how the ball gets even bigger above your head.

Now bring the energy from the ball above your head into your body, through the top of your head, through your crown chakra. See it filling your whole body. Feel it filling up your arms and your legs.

Now you are going to bring energy up from the earth through your root chakra, which is at the bottom of your tailbone, where you sit on the floor. You may see this energy as a color. Feel earth energy come up out of the ground, up through the bottom of the building, all the way through the floor where you are sitting. Can you hear it? Feel this energy come up through the floor and into your body. If you want, ask the animals and plants of the earth to help you. Watch these animals sending energy to you from the earth through your root chakra at your tailbone.

Now see the earth energy mixing with the light ball energy in your body, which might be like mixing chocolate syrup into vanilla ice cream. I will give you a moment to really feel this energy mixing in your body. Remember, the energy from the stars and from the earth never run out, so you can continue to see the energies from above and below come into your body.

I'll give you a few moments to do this on your own.

Now thank yourself for all the good feelings you brought

into your body today. *(Pause.)* You can open your eyes whenever you are ready.

After Meditation Questions

1. What did you see?
2. How did you feel? What did it sound like?
3. Did you get some help from the stars and the animals?
4. What good energies did you put into the ball of energy above your head?
5. What did the earth energy look like?

Huna Technique

Heartache affects us physically, mentally, and emotionally. When we lose someone, whether it is because of death or disagreement, we *feel* sad. We *think* about our actions and often *feel* physical pain in our chest.

This meditation is inspired by a technique used in Huna, an ancient spiritual practice from Hawaii. You probably have heard of a Kahuna, which is a Huna master, usually specializing in a particular ability. People who practice Huna believe energetic cords connect us to all the people we have relationships with, whether the relationship is with a family member, a classmate, or someone we met on the street. Huna practitioners believe that if these cords are cut in meditation, then hard feelings on either end of the cord will be released. As soon as either person sees or thinks of the other, the cords are reunited in a new connection that offers a fresh perspective on the relationship, especially if the effort is made not to slip back into old relationship patterns.

The Huna technique that inspired this meditation is called *ho'o pono pono*, which means "to make right." This ancient practice involves forgiveness, which is a wonderful concept to teach your child. Forgiveness means that we love someone no matter what, that we understand what happened from the other person's point of view, and that we have taken time to forgive ourselves and give ourselves what we need to heal. Some people believe there are no accidents or coincidences. In this case, forgiveness means to invite our higher self to show us the big picture so we understand why the hurtful situation came about.

This journey meditation is for children eight years old and older. The imagery could be adjusted easily for younger children. This experience is perfect for getting through teen breakups or resolving conflicts between your child and his classmates, friends, or family members.

~HEALING HEART MEDITATION~

Before doing this meditation, ask your child to choose a person in his life with whom he has had a disagreement, or someone who hurt his feelings.

Close your eyes. You can put your hands over your eyes if you want to. Now take a deep in-breath. When you breathe back out, feel your body relaxing. We'll take two more breaths. Deep breath in, and relax your legs as you breathe out. Deep breath in, and relax your arms and neck as you breathe out.

Imagine a beautiful stage. This might be like the stage in your school auditorium or like a stage in a movie theater. Or it may be something completely different: whatever comes to your mind. Notice seats in front of the stage. You are on the stage, and there are people in the audience. They are all of the people you know: your family, everyone in your school, all your teachers, and the people who live in your neighborhood. They are all there. Even if you don't see them, you know they are there.

The person you picked before the meditation is in the audience. Invite this person to come on stage with you. Now think of a time when you were upset with this person, or sad because of something this person said or did. Let yourself feel all the feelings you felt when that happened. *(Pause.)*

Now I would like you to tell this person how you feel. If you feel sad, tell them that, and if you feel afraid, tell them that as well. If you feel angry, tell them what makes you angry.

Now I would like you to see a stream of energy coming out of your heart and going into this person's heart. Feel a soft, gentle energy moving from your heart into this person's heart. You might see this energy as a color. Also see a soft, gentle energy coming out of this person's heart and into yours. This is healing energy you share with one another. Take a moment to feel this stream of energy between you. You might even hear the energy moving.

Now see the energy change to a different color. This new energy is forgiveness energy, which flows from your heart into this person's heart, and from this person's heart into yours. Feel this energy flowing between you.

Thank this person for being here with you today and sharing the healing and forgiveness energy with you.

Now float above the stage so you are looking down on this person with whom you have just shared healing and forgiveness energy. You might see the top of their head, or this person might be looking up at you. Now see a long ribbon tied around you. The other end of this ribbon is tied to the person below you on the stage. Feel yourself connected to them by the ribbon.

Now cut the ribbon with a safe pair of scissors and float away from the person, above the stage. You are now disconnected and free to float up and outside of the building—far and away into the clouds above. In these clouds, there is a perfect place with all of your favorite things. See yourself playing quietly with one of your favorite toys or doing something else you enjoy doing quietly on your own. I'll give you a few moments to enjoy your cloud.

Now thank yourself for all your good work *(Pause.)* You can open your eyes whenever you are ready.

After Meditation Questions
1. What did you see and feel when you shared the healing and forgiveness energy?
2. What did you do on your cloud?
3. Did you feel safe and happy?

CONTEMPLATIVE PRAYER

Imagine you are with your loved one, sitting in front of a fireplace. You are deeply enjoying each other's company. You sense with certainty that this person loves you, while you feel the fire warm your body. Both you and your loved one are completely quiet, which is appropriate because no words exist to describe your experience.

Let us use this scene to understand *contemplative prayer.*

When practicing contemplative prayer, this person sitting with you in front of the fire is God. When specifically practicing Christian contemplative prayer, this person is Christ. When we practice contemplative prayer, we do not imagine the warm fireplace, although the feeling is similar. Instead, we sit still, close our eyes, and invite God into our hearts. One definition of contemplative prayer is being alone with God, who we know loves us. Contemplative prayer is also commonly referred to as *prayer of faith, prayer of the heart, prayer of simplicity, prayer of simple regard,* and *active quiet.*

Contemplative practice and Christian meditation should not be confused—they are quite different. *Contemplative prayer* involves quieting the mind, while Christian meditation, or *discursive meditation,* uses thought and imagination to better understand God. For example, we might meditate on a question or affirmation. Conversely, Buddhists define these two terms in an opposite fashion. Buddhists say that *contemplation* means intentional thought (similar to Christian meditation) and *meditation* means quieting the mind (similar to contemplative prayer). These two terms had confused me for years, until my meditation mentor pointed out the flip-flop use of these words within these two traditions.

When practicing contemplative prayer, we might use discursive meditation to help us ease into contemplation. And we might even toggle back and forth between contemplative prayer and meditation in one sitting.

The objective of contemplative prayer is to fully merge with God's will, completely leaving our own will behind. Stages of contemplative prayer are delineated by how much of our will we let go of and how much of God's will we embody. Achieving a state of total expression of God's will can be compared to a Buddhist attaining enlightenment. What links these two outcomes is an exercise of total surrender of *self* (as defined by Buddhists).

When high levels of surrender are accomplished, reasoning is largely replaced with intuition and thoughts manifest in the simplest form. In my opinion, this state offers children a tool with which to glide through life with more ease and grace. A real-life example of this is a child who becomes upset over not getting what she is fixated on receiving. We can teach this child that the solution is not getting that *thing*, but rather becoming a *mind ninja* who is capable of letting go of thoughts that lead her to believe that she must have the object. The conversation might go like this:

Holly is very upset because I have told her she cannot play her video game right now. She is so angry that she throws objects across the room. I engage the child with this conversation:

"Can you change your mind about wanting to play your video game right now?" I propose.

"No."

"Why not?" I ask.

"Because I don't want to."

"Can you change your mind about not wanting to?"

"I don't want to."

She is yelling, crying, and reaching for more items to throw. I continue, "What would help you calm down so you can let go of your thoughts about wanting to play the video game?"

The child lies down, clutching a stuffed animal, but still visibly upset. She has decided the stuffed animal will help her calm down.

I suggest: "Can you give your thoughts about playing your video game to God? They seem too big and heavy for you to keep inside."

If a child practices contemplative prayer, then it will become easier for her to give up her concerns and let God inside her heart. Her fixation on needing the item will lessen and her thoughts about needing the item will become less influential.

~PRAYER OF THE HEART MEDITATION~

Contemplative prayer can be practiced in a variety of ways. Some practitioners inhale slowly and deeply through their noses as they count to five. Then they hold the breath for a moment and finally breathe back out through their mouths gradually while counting to five. Others begin with discursive meditation, placing their attention lightly on a Bible verse, affirmation, pleasant scene, or even a question. Their attention is similar to gazing at a beautiful flower—not thinking about the details of the flower or trying to decide whether to pluck the flower from its stem; but instead simply noticing its beauty instead.

In the following meditation, I will use a third method for entering contemplative meditation, which is based on *centering prayer*. Centering prayer is a specific type of contemplative prayer taught by Catholic Trappist monks. Before beginning the meditation, have the child choose a sacred word to use during her meditation. Christian examples include *Amen, Christ, Jesus,* and *Abba.* More universal words include *peace, grace, trust,* and *love.* Similar to *Me and My Mantra* meditation in Chapter 8, the child can choose any word as long as it fills the purpose, which is either to help her relax or to help her feel closer to God.

Close your eyes. You can put your hands over your eyes if you want to. Now take a deep breath in. When you breathe back out, feel your body relaxing.

Say your sacred word silently in your head. Notice how quiet you are. If you hear yourself begin to say words in your head, say your sacred word silently. Then notice how quiet you are inside once again.

You don't have to say your sacred word over and over; just say it when you need to become quiet or if you start thinking about something. You can even use your sacred word to make what I am saying sound softer.

(Pause.) Speak more softly. Depending on your religious faith, include these next three sentences.

A part of God dwells in each one of us. Imagine that Jesus is small enough to sit inside your heart. See him smiling at you from inside your heart.

Feel your heart grow big and bright. You might feel your heart grow, or you might see bright light all around your chest. Feel how much God loves you. Then use your big, bright heart to love God back.

If you start to think about other things at any time during this meditation, simply say your sacred word. I will let you do this on your own. (*Pause.*)

You did a great job quieting your thoughts and letting God love you. Open your eyes whenever you are ready.

After Meditation Questions
1. Did your sacred word help you become quiet inside?
2. What did your heart feel like?
3. Do you feel like God is next to you?
4. Is it easier for you to remember God when you are quiet?

MORE FUN BEFORE AND AFTER THE MEDITATIONS

"Meditation Has a First Name" Song
Sing the following song to the "Oscar Mayer Weiner" jingle.

Meditation has a first name,
It's f-e-e-l-i-n-g.
Meditation has a second name,
It's s-e-e-i-n-g.

I love to meditate every day,

And if you ask me why . . . I'll say,

Meditation likes to help me hear-see-feel ev-ery-thing.

"Hug Monster" Game

You will need at least four participants for this activity. Have each child take a turn being the Hug Monster. The Hug Monster has five seconds to hug as many people as he can. The object is to see how many hugs can accumulate for the whole group. Add up each child's hug score for a final group hug score. You can count *one-one thousand, two-one thousand* or use a stop watch to time the Hug Monster. If fewer than five children are present, ask the children to stand further apart from each other and stay in their places. This will make it more challenging for the Hug Monster, who can move around to give as many hugs as possible.

"My Favorite Thing to Do" Charade

Ask your child to think about some of his favorite things to do and ask him to act out one of them. Then guess what he is acting out. This helps your child remember what activities and feelings nourish his soul.

Art Projects

1. Have your child draw a picture of something he experienced during meditation.

2. Find a box at least 11 by 16 inches, with short sides for catching glitter. Have your child draw his ball of energy from the "Fudge Swirl" meditation on a piece of paper with crayon or marker. Then ask him to decorate his energy ball with a glue stick or bottle of liquid glue, and place the paper in the box. Have him sprinkle glitter across the paper and shake the paper back and forth, allowing the glitter to cover the glue completely. Then carefully shake off the remaining glitter and set the paper aside to dry.

3. Have your child create a collage of things that nourish his soul.

Offer magazines from which he can cut pictures and words, or give him yarn, cotton balls, construction paper, stickers, and anything else you have available for him to paste into his collage.

4. Have your child pretend he is a king (a queen if you have a daughter). Explain to him that he gets to do all his favorite things in his kingdom. Have him paint pictures of himself in his kingdom.

Writing Activity

If your child is old enough, ask him to write a letter, poem, or song for the person with whom he shared forgiveness and healing energy in his meditation.

chapter 11

INNER WORLDS

WHAT MAKES ME HAPPY? What are my needs? Where did I come from? Where am I going? are all questions your child can better answer with meditation. The guided imagery experiences shared in this chapter help a child delve into the depths of his own consciousness and uncover truths about himself.

Since human consciousness is so vast and abstract, most people do not investigate this part of themselves. However, the truth is, the symbolic world within plays an important role in driving our actions. When we work with our *inner worlds* we can address personal challenges and lead happier lives. Carl Jung, who studied with Sigmund Freud, believed that archetypes are specific energies within our unconscious, which greatly influence who we are. When children meet archetypal energies in meditation, the energies present themselves in different forms: perhaps as animals or even as characters from a storybook. Children can overcome obstacles they face when they work with these forms during meditation.

Below are two examples of how meditation allows children to access and benefit from deeper dimensions of their consciousness.

> Ryan's mother notices he has been sad for the last three days. During "The Happy Tree" meditation, Ryan sees a tree with both happy and sad fruit dangling from the branches. This fruit represents two different aspects of himself. His sad fruit tell him they want hugs, bedtime stories, and a trip to Grandma's.

Since meditating, Ryan has a better awareness of his emotional needs. *Why* Ryan is sad might not be solved in this particular sitting, but that could be the object of future meditations.

During the "Inside Friends" meditation, Raquel's *listening part* of herself gives her a gift. On unwrapping it she finds a pretty purple pillow with her name sewn onto it. Her Listener tells her this pillow is a special place for Raquel to sit when she wants to be quiet and listen to her heart. Raquel now knows it is important for her well-being to welcome heart-centered guidance.

When we create space for all our essences to be heard, we learn about ourselves. Although these aspects are abstract, the experiences we have with them are concrete and profound. Your child will have no doubts as to their reality.

In this chapter, I offer a meditation that helps a child take a step back and observe his feelings and give whatever drives these feelings a chance to express their needs. In addition, included is a journey meditation that allows a child to meet and take guidance from his archetypal essences. I also share a fun meditation that leads a child to witness possible pasts and futures. When children unlock the secrets of what motivates their behavior, they can overcome personal challenges with ease.

SYMBOLIC JOURNEYING

Happiness is a simple, beautiful word that touches all of us at the very core. What makes you happy? What makes you unhappy? We are conscious of many activities, people, foods, feelings, events, and so on that make us happy. At the same time, we are not always conscious of what brings us happiness. For example, Elena, mother of three, is so busy running around keeping up with her daily activities and weekly commitments that she doesn't realize that, deep down inside, a part of her wants to take off for a day and go to an amusement park, which would make her feel happy and joyous, like a child. In meditation, we can become aware of unconscious needs that lead to happiness.

The following meditation is one I conceived on the spot one day during a private session with a ten-year-old girl who was having trouble understanding her feelings about her parents' recent divorce. This quick and easy meditation was so successful I have since used it in countless sessions with other children to help them understand themselves more fully.

In this meditation, your child will communicate with unhappy aspects of herself and find out what brings her happiness. The answers she will see, hear, and feel might be symbolic, but as noted previously, you can decide whether to enjoy the symbolism without analyzing it or whether to ask your child to offer her own interpretation.

~THE HAPPY TREE MEDITATION~

Close your eyes. You can put your hands over your eyes if you want to. Now take a deep in-breath. When you breathe back out, feel your body relaxing. We'll take two more breaths. Deep breath in, and relax your legs as you breathe out. Deep breath in, and relax your arms and neck as you breathe out.

Imagine a tree. The tree has fruit on it. The tree can have any kind of fruit you want. Do you see the fruit? Some of the fruits are happy and some are sad. The happy ones are different from the sad ones. Can you tell which are sad?

Ask the sad fruits, "Sad fruit, what do you need to be happy?" Listen quietly. Can you hear them speaking to you? Do they want to go somewhere or do they need something? *(Pause.)* Great, do that for them. *(Pause.)* How do the fruits feel now? Now look at the tree. How does the tree feel? Does the tree need anything? (*Pause.*) Good, help the tree with that. (*Pause.*)

See the sun shining down on the tree. Feel the rays of the sun helping the tree. Put some of your favorite things into the sun. What would you like to put into the sun? Smiles, love, fun, maybe your favorite toy? Okay, go ahead and put some things that make you feel good into the sun. You may see these things as a color or a picture, or maybe they make sounds. Take in a deep breath. As you take in this breath, feel the good energy from the sun going into the tree. Take another deep breath and see more good energy going into the tree.

We're almost done. Now thank the tree and yourself for all your great work. (*Pause.*) You can open your eyes whenever you are ready.

After Meditation Questions

1. How do you feel? Do you feel different?
2. How did the sad fruit look different from the happy fruit?
3. What did the sad fruit need?
4. What did the good energy look or sound like?
5. Do you think this meditation is helpful?
6. Do you think you could do this meditation on your own?

ARCHETYPES

Our consciousness is a complex pool of emotions, thoughts, archetypal energies, and more. We can become aware of these essences when we take a moment to tune in to them. When we create a loving space for all our essences to be heard, we become whole. The following journey meditation will help your child become aware of his archetypal energies and their needs. The meditation is loosely based on Carl Jung's archetypes. These archetypes include the part of ourselves that likes to have fun, the part that likes to play sports, the part that likes to be loud, and the part that likes to be quiet—just to name a few.

Seven-year-old Luis benefits from connecting with his archetypal energies. He loves to have fun and escaped through his front door whenever he had a chance. Unfortunately, he often found himself in precarious situations. You could have found him climbing in areas he had been told were unsafe. You could have seen him running into the street after imaginary vicious dragons, for example. Although Luis was having fun, his parents were worried for his safety.

Luis's mother led him through a meditation during which he met his *fun-seeking* essence or archetype. Luis asked this essence what he needed to be happy. This Robin Hood-like figure told Luis, "I want more playtime with Daddy."

Luis has used meditation to become conscious of one of his archetypal energies. As a result, Luis and his parents become aware of why he finds it challenging to follow safety suggestions. With a few shifts in routine, such as Luis's father carving out more time for his son, Luis becomes more careful and aware of safety. His fun-seeking essence has been heard, and his needs are now being met.

This meditation introduces your child to the part of herself that likes to listen and the part that likes to do things; however, any of the following archetypal pairs can be used instead. Jungian psychologists speak of the Warrior, the Parental Figure, the Artist, and other archetypes. I like to present these concepts to children in ways that they will resonate with easily. Feel free to create more appropriate ones for your child.

ARCHETYPE PAIRS

- ~ The Listener and the Doer (used in the following meditation)
- ~ The Thrill-Seeking Tiger and the Cautious Cat

- ˜ The Bookworm and the Athlete
- ˜ The Wizard/Dreamer and the Practical Thinker
- ˜ The Wise Woman/Man and the Young Child
- ˜ The Loud Drum and the Quiet Feather
- ˜ The Teacher and the Student

These pairs often work together, especially the Listener and the Doer. In this meditation, quiet, timid children gain more confidence to act on their inner voices, while very active children gain the ability to *listen* more to their inner voices rather than acting unconsciously. Before this meditation, I suggest you and your child do the "Listening to My Teddy Bear" activity at the end of this chapter. This experience will help her practice listening to her inner voice.

~INSIDE FRIENDS MEDITATION~

Close your eyes. You can put your hands over your eyes if you want to. Now take a deep in-breath. When you breathe back out, feel your body relaxing. We'll take two more breaths. Deep breath in, and relax your legs as you breathe out. Deep breath in, and relax your arms and neck as you breathe out.

I would like you to imagine yourself in one of your favorite places. It doesn't matter where you are, just as long as you like being there. I want you to see the Listener part of yourself playing with you. Notice what it feels like to be near your Listener. You might see this part of yourself as an animal or a special character, or your Listener might look just like you, like a twin. While you are there with the Listener, ask them what they need to be happy. *(Pause.)* What did your Listener tell you? Is there anything you want to tell your Listener? *(Pause.)*

Now I want you to see the Doer part of yourself playing with both you and the Listener. Your Doer might be an animal or a special character, or might look just like you. While you are there with the Doer, ask them what they need to be happy. *(Pause.)* What did the Doer tell you? Is there anything you want to tell the Doer? *(Pause.)*

Your Doer and Listener have presents for you. Open your hands to receive the presents. If they are wrapped, unwrap them and see what they are. *(Pause.)* Give your Listener and Doer a great big hug, and thank them for spending time with you today in your meditation.

When you are done talking with your Listener and Doer, go ahead and open your eyes.

After Meditation Questions
1. What did your Listener and Doer look like?
2. What did your Listener say she needed to be happy?
3. What did your Doer say she needed to be happy?
4. What presents did they give you? Why do you think they gave you those presents instead of something else?

REGRESSION

This meditation is a favorite among my school-aged students. They love using their inner senses to see colorful, faraway lands, and hear the voices and sounds within these lands. It is a wonderful opportunity for them to feel the textures and even emotions sparked by these mysterious journeys.

Children love this meditation, too; I think because it helps them access deep, often hidden thoughts and emotions. Because of the profound experiences this meditation can release, I offer some brief information about the subconscious, past lives, and interpreting the future. Whether children are actually tapping in to their pasts and futures, I am not always sure. But these perspectives might be helpful.

As we have seen, meditation allows us to access our subconscious, which holds all of our memories. The conscious mind is our waking mind, what we think about in the present moment. A computer is a good metaphor for the conscious and subconscious: the subconscious mind is the hard drive where all our files are stored, while the thoughts of the conscious mind are the open files on the desktop. Through techniques such as meditation, we can close certain files and open others, becoming conscious of memories we may not otherwise have been aware of.

The "Time Machine" meditation can bring up unusual experiences with helpful consequences. Some people believe that during meditation we can get in touch with memories from our past lives. The psychiatrist Dr. Brian Weiss wrote a popular book entitled *Many Lives, Many Masters*, a passionate story about his regression work with Catherine, a 27-year-old client.[1] Catherine suffered from anxiety, panic attacks, and phobias that left her emotionally paralyzed. Most of her conditions related to her fear of water and of choking to death. During their 18 months of working together, Weiss helped Catherine reconnect with childhood memories that involved her gagging and choking, and with three past lives (1863 BC, 1586 BC, and 1756 AD), which all ended with her being choked by water. Weiss reports that his client's fears of water and choking diminished after she connected with these memories.

Dr. Weiss helped his client access her subconscious memories. Although there is some debate about the origin of these memories, most agree the memories are situated in the subconscious. These ideas are abstract, and it is difficult to know exactly where memories are "located." But in any case, when we uncover them we gain an understanding of ourselves that is deeply healing.

Dr. Weiss and Catherine's intense experience is a well-known

example of how regression in a meditative state can heal one emotionally. Carol Bowman expands on this relating to children in her
book *Children's Past Lives*. Bowman tells her extraordinary story of
her son and daughter's past life memories. Both her children overcame
troubling phobias. Her five-year-old son, terrified by loud noises,
recalled a former life as a black man who fired cannons during the
civil war. His detailed wartime memories were verified by a historian.
How encouraging to find that her children enjoyed connecting to past
life memories despite the intensity of these memories. I was inspired
to learn Bowman's two children were both healed immediately after
finding their past-life connections.

In her book, Bowman covers the work of Dr. Ian Stevenson,
former psychiatrist, researcher and department head at University of
Virginia. He traveled the world documenting cases in which children
between two and four years old spontaneously revealed enough clues
about *another life* that their former identity was established. Stevenson's
thorough investigation excluded cases that could be explained by any
other means.[2]

In one case, three-year-old Swarnlata asked her family to turn
down a road a hundred miles from her home so they could get a better
cup of tea at "her house." Swarnlata launched into many details about
"her life" including her full name Biya Pathak, descriptions of her
house and surroundings, and how she died. Seven years later, with the
help of another researcher, they found the house and family Swarnlata
described.

When Swarnlata reunited with the Pathak's, she recognized and
named all family members, commented on changes to the property
since Biya's death, and revealed the location of a box of money that only
Mr. Pathak and his former wife Biya knew about. This is one of 2,600
cases Stevenson investigated in which children were reunited with
people and places revealed in their spontaneous *past life memories*.

Whether you believe in reincarnation or not, the stories children share about where they come from are astounding. One of my adult students who had lost her brother Thomas nine years earlier, shared with me that her three-year-old son told her, "I know what happened to Uncle Thomas when he died. His spirit left his body and went into your body and came out as me." This was especially remarkable considering she had never talked to her son about this possibility or about reincarnation.

Many people believe we reincarnate into the same family we left when we died. It is said that families hold deep soul connections, and family members choose to go through many lives together to help each other experience what they came here to learn. One parent shared that his five-year-old daughter told him, "I remember when I was big and you were little." With the vocabulary she had at the time, this was how she explained to her father that she remembered when she was the adult and he was the child, possibly her child.

Some also believe that when a child comes into the world, she consciously chooses her parents before conception. She makes this choice based on what experiences she wishes to have during her life. Another student shared with me that her four-year-old daughter told her, "There were so many mommies to choose from, but you had the nicest smile."

For some people, the following meditation can bring memories from a previously lived past into consciousness, but this certainly does not always happen. In fact, many children project themselves into the future, while more adults access the past during this meditation. After all, children do not occupy themselves with the past the way we adults do. They seem to be more interested in their futures.

Seeing into the future could be considered prediction, obviously, and prediction of the future brings up several questions. Is our future static or dynamic? Does it change with every thought and decision we make? Or do we rely on fate? Personally, I do not believe that we can predict the future, but we can see and explore possible outcomes based on our patterns of thought and actions. In other words, the future is not fixed, but a dynamic combination of elements. Patterns can easily change, especially if we are motivated to change them.

This meditation will help your child better understand who she is today by visiting possible pasts and futures. This meditation can help her find root causes for fears. Great healing can take place when children connect with a significant moment in a past life memory such as their death. If nothing else, this journey is an exciting adventure—an alternative to TV and video games. This meditation is a sure favorite with my students.

~TIME MACHINE MEDITATION~

Close your eyes. You can put your hands over your eyes if you want to. Now take a deep in-breath. When you breathe back out, feel your body relaxing. We'll take two more breaths. Deep breath in, and relax your legs as you breathe out. Deep breath in, and relax your arms and neck as you breathe out.

See a time machine with a door on it. Your time machine can look like anything you choose, like a big box or a car or a building, for example. Now open the door to the time machine and step inside. Go ahead and make sure the door is closed when you are inside. Once inside, you might see different kinds of controls and lights. Notice what it feels like in your machine. Look around inside your time machine. You might even want to put a seatbelt on. There is a switch that turns the time machine on, so make sure the switch is turned to On.

The time machine already knows where to take you, whether that is in the past or the future. Now find the button that tells the machine to take you to this already set perfect time for you to visit, and press that button. Feel the time machine switch into gear. It might make loud noises or even shake a bit. Relax and enjoy the ride.

When the time machine has brought you to the perfect time, go ahead and unhook the seat belt and open the door to this new time and place. First notice the ground. What does it feel like under your feet? Look at your feet. What kind of shoes do you have on, if any? Take a look at your hands and arms. Touch your arms. Are you *you* or are you in a different body? Take a look at what is around you. Are you in a place where there are buildings? Or are you in nature? Listen. What do you hear? You might feel drawn to a certain area, so go ahead and move to that area. Are there any people around? If you feel comfortable asking them where you are, go ahead and ask them. If there are not any people, go ahead and ask an invisible guide who is there with you. What year is it? Where am I? *(Pause.)* You can also ask what you need to see in this place, and let yourself be guided to whatever you need to see. *(Pause.)*

When you feel ready to leave this place, go back to the time machine and go inside. Turn the machine on, fasten your seatbelt, and set the control dial to the present time. Then push the button that will begin your journey home. Sit back and enjoy the ride.

When you return, open the door and move out of the machine. Now thank yourself for all the things you saw on your travels. *(Pause.)* You can open your eyes whenever you are ready.

After Meditation Questions

1. What did you see?
2. Did someone guide you and answer your questions?
3. What were you wearing?
4. What year did you go to?

STUDENTS ENJOY THE TIME MACHINE MEDITATION

Angela, a child meditation facilitator, leads her meditation class through the *Time Machine meditation*. Afterwards, her students begin to stir, shifting their limbs and pushing themselves into more upright positions. The room is still and almost completely silent. Angela gazes at the awakening children and then asks them to share what they heard, felt, and saw during their meditation.

One boy shares: "I was in a garden with bricks on the ground. I went to a fountain. I scooped up water from the fountain and put it into a bottle. I did this because it made me feel better. I don't know how to explain it."

One of the girls in the class says: "I don't know where I went, but it was nighttime and I was a little girl. I sat beside a man I did not know. I asked him, 'Why am I here?' He answered, 'Just to get away.' It felt good."

Her twin sister speaks up next: "I found myself in my backyard. I saw my grandmother reach out to me." The young meditator is filled with emotion. Her voice begins to crack. "I looked down and noticed that I was in water. I was in our pool that I used to swim in all the time. Just talking to my grandmother and being able to see her in front of me, moving and standing up straight by herself, made me feel so good."

The girl's head falls into her hands. She wipes the tears away with her fingers. "My grandmother told me to always be strong," she adds. This message strikes a cord with her twin sister, who also shares her sister's emotion. Their younger sister and her friend, who sit on the floor a few feet in front of them, turn around to take in this energy that no one can quite explain.

The tone is tender, as everyone in the room holds affection for the moment. Attention gradually shifts to someone else, who paints an enchanting picture of a forest leading to a waterfall. She says: "I walked barefooted to the waterfall, where I saw deer and rabbits. An angel came out from the waterfall and said to me that I've done really well letting go of my great grandpa and I should keep going." She hugs her knees and drops her head. Angela reaches over to comfort her. The class is silent for several moments.

Another student says: "I saw God and heard that I need to remember that I am an amazing writer. And that I should walk with my light and not feel alone."

The last boy passes the opportunity to share. Maybe he is consumed, considering the stories before him. Maybe he is contemplating his own inner journey and will be ready to talk about it later. Or maybe his story is his alone to experience. Whatever it is, no one puts any pressure on him to speak.

MORE FUN BEFORE AND AFTER THE MEDITATIONS

"Tree People" Movement Game

Have your child pretend she is a tree. Ask her to pretend her arms are tree branches. Then ask her to pretend her feet are tree roots digging into the ground. Explain that you are the wind, the rain, and the sunshine. Play out these weather conditions, or choose a student to do so if you are working with a group. Encourage your child to close her eyes while you blow like the wind and flutter about like raindrops. Your child can sway in the wind, feel wet in the rain, and blossom in the sun.

Listening to My Teddy Bear

This activity helps children understand the concept of listening to themselves. Explain to your child that for today, when you use the word *listen* you do not mean "listening to Mom or Dad." Instead you mean "listening to yourself." Ask her if she can share with you a time when she heard herself.

Next, place an object in front of your child—like a stuffed animal or a plant—something with which a child can communicate. Ask her to close her eyes and say to the teddy bear or plant, "How do you feel today?" or "What is your favorite food?" or any question she wishes to ask. If there is more than one child, encourage the children to ask their questions silently and to raise their hands when they have heard their answers. When all the children have raised their hands, tell them to open their eyes. Then have each child share what she heard.

What Does It Look Like Where You Are?

Make three large squares on the floor, about three by three feet, using masking tape or three blankets laid out on the floor. Designate one blanket as "The Future," another as "The Present," and the third as "The Past." Have your child jump into whichever square she chooses. Then ask her to close her eyes, while you say, "You are in The Future. What does it look like?" Give her a few moments of quiet time in the square to access her imagination and tell you what she sees, hears, and feels.

Art Projects

1. Have your child make a collage from magazines and construction paper of something she saw in meditation.

2. Have your child make puppets of her Listener and Doer. They can be made out of paper lunch bags or socks. Your child can glue items on to her sock puppets, or draw and color on the paper bag puppets.

3. If your child is old enough, have her make a book with pictures

of the presents given her by the Listener and Doer, including an explanation of the meaning of the gifts or why she was given these items. Pictures of significant objects seen in other meditations can also be added.

4. Find a huge box; a refrigerator box is best. Help your child transform the box into a time machine. Use paints, paper, aluminum foil, and other materials to make a spectacular vehicle for time travel.

5. Help your child make the clothing and hats she wore in her "Time Machine" meditation. Use fabric, construction paper, yarn, markers, and whatever else is handy. Have dress-up clothes available. If you have time, encourage your child to play out her experience in front of family or friends.

chapter 12

CREATING NEW MEDITATIONS

THE MEDITATIONS IN THE PREVIOUS FOUR CHAPTERS will help your child enhance his mental, emotional, physical, and spiritual health, as well as help him know himself more deeply. Although these meditations address the core issues that most children experience, you might not find a meditation that specifically addresses your child's current challenge. Not to worry. This chapter gives you two different methods for creating effective meditations that target your child's unique needs and personal interests.

The first method involves asking your child questions about his challenge and the feelings it brings up. This method utilizes metaphors to help him resolve his issue. The second technique is a meditation exercise for parents and educators. This process allows you to experience the world through a child's eyes, which will help you understand what elements are important to include when writing an original meditation. Knowing how to create personalized meditations for your child is invaluable.

CREATING METAPHORICAL JOURNEYS

Imagine your child has come home from school for the sixth time this month complaining about one of his classmates. His feelings are hurt once again, and it sounds like his classmate's feelings are hurt also. You've guided him twice through the "Healing Heart" meditation from Chapter 10, which was helpful, but your child is still having a difficult time with his classmate. Creating a special meditation for him that specifically addresses his situation will probably be just what he needs.

The following process will make use of your child's favorite TV character, sport, or other interest, in a meditation journey that draws him more completely into the experience and provides a metaphor for his issue. When he shares with you the elements of his favorite TV show, storybook, movie, or sport, it is not imperative that you know anything about this show or sport. How your child interprets the story and character or the athletic event is more important than the actual content of the show or athletic activity.

In one of the following steps, you will ask your child what it looks like when he feels a certain way. Surprisingly, children can answer this abstract question quite easily. Our subconscious minds can quickly give us a metaphor for how we experience an emotion, and children in particular locate these metaphors with ease.

In another step, you will ask your child what he thinks needs to happen to solve the issue. This question follows the exchange about what his emotions look like, and therefore, it is possible that his solution will be symbolic. His symbolism will not only help you when you compose his meditation, but it will also give you both some insight into how best to help him find a resolution.

Confused? Don't worry. The process is actually quite easy. The inclusion of your child's favorite character or other passion, a metaphor for his feelings, and his suggestions for a solution combine to form the recipe for a fun and successful meditation journey.

The following are guidelines for developing this metaphorical journey, including a sample dialogue from an actual session I had with an eight-year-old client, Miguel.

1. Talk to your child about the issue. Ask him questions until you have a good understanding of the problem and its causes.

Guide: How was school today?

Miguel: I got mad because people around me did things to get me upset. There is this one kid in my class named Christo who is always bothering me.

Guide: What did you do when Christo upset you?

Miguel: I punched him.

Guide: What feelings do you feel when this happens?

Miguel: I feel like something takes over my brain and is controlling it.

Guide: What does that look like?

Miguel: It looks like a light and a switch in my head that turns on when I get mad.

Guide: What color is it?

Miguel: The light is green and the switch is blue.

Guide: What does it sound like?

Miguel: Click and buzzing.

2. Find out what your child thinks needs to happen to solve the problem, and focus on the visual description he gave you in step 1. Word your questions so as to help him give you useful answers. Or give suggestions until you find a solution he agrees with.

Guide: What needs to happen to the switch to help you feel less mad?

Miguel: The switch needs to be turned back.

3. Ask questions to learn your child's interests and what he relates to; for example, ask questions about a TV show, movie, hobby, storybook, or sport. The answers to these questions will help you prepare a guided experience that will excite your child.

Find out the parameters of the show or movie. Parameters are the principles and rules of the story. For example, the parameters of Superman are that he comes to earth from another planet with special powers. Superman can fly and demonstrate supernatural strength; however, when he is near kryptonite, his powers are slowly taken away and eventually he becomes powerless. You can find out these details by asking questions like "What is this movie about? What happens in this TV show?" Also ask who the child's favorite character is in the story, so you know who he relates to most.

Guide: What is your favorite movie or TV show?

Miguel: Scooby Doo.

Guide: What happens during your Scooby Doo shows?

Miguel: All kinds of things. Shaggy and Scooby and Fred and their friends go to Skull Island to look for clues. They solve mysteries like the mystery of the Cat Creature.

Guide: What do Shaggy and Scooby find on Skull Island?

Miguel: Ghosts and torpedoes and an underground mansion.

Guide: What do you like about these shows?

Miguel: I like it when the Cat Creature steals the jewels and they find out he's really Daphne's Aunt's Doctor. (This answer helps us understand the parameters of the show. Mystery solving is an important parameter.)

The Guide: Who is your favorite character in Scooby Doo?

Miguel: Shaggy and Scooby.

4. Let your imagination run wild. Think up a story through which to guide your child that plays upon the motifs in his favorite movie or another interest that you talked about. Make sure your story prompts your child to visualize and resolve his conflict. He can *be* the main character or *watch* the character play out the scenario in his mind. Let the meditation come together quickly. Consider including the following criteria, but don't get distracted by them.

   A. Create a scene with your child's favorite characters or other interest.

   B. Lead your child to experience the problem.

   C. Guide him to visualize his emotions.

D. Incorporate your child's solution.

E. Leave him in a comfortable place.

Fresh, spontaneous adventures are most successful. Just begin talking, and effortlessly allow the perfect meditation journey to come alive. Here is an example of a meditation for Miguel incorporating the five criteria.

Close your eyes and take a deep in-breath. When you breathe back out, let your body feel sleepy.

(A) Let's pretend you are spending the day with Shaggy and Scooby. You are on a boat with them headed for a haunted island. Can you *hear* the engine of the boat? Normally Shaggy and Scooby are the best of friends but today they are getting frustrated with each other. Let's look for clues to help Shaggy and Scooby figure out how to become friends again.

You reach the island and pull the boat up on the shore. You can put your hands through the sand and *feel* it brush through your fingers. Oh look, do you *see* the footprints in the sand? I think they belong to the Cat Creature. This must be your first clue. You, Shaggy and Scooby follow the footprints. You are still following the footprints. Oh, look where they end. There is a control box lying in the sand. The Cat Creature must have left it there.

(B) Shaggy picks up the box and then Scooby tries to pull it away from Shaggy.

(C) You notice the two of them getting pretty angry with each other while they pull the box back and forth. Then a green light on the box turns on, and you hear a buzzing sound.

(D) You have an idea. Tell Scooby and Shaggy to take three long deep breaths. Ready one... two... three. And then help Scooby and Shaggy turn the blue switch off on the control box. Both Shaggy and Scooby feel much better.

(E) You are all very happy that together you solved the mystery of how Shaggy and Scooby can become friends again. Scooby and Shaggy thank you for your help and let you know that next time they get into an argument they will take deep breaths and turn the blue switch back. Now it is time for you, Shaggy and Scooby ride your boat back home.

This is a simple yet powerful adventure your child can easily experience. Since it incorporates his favorite characters, the child will be excited and focused on his inner adventure. He might even request to do it again. In this example, I have Miguel spend time with the characters he enjoys while these characters feel emotions of frustration and then resolve them. Although Miguel suggests that they take three deep breaths, Miguel does not experience the cool down himself. If I thought Miguel should experience the emotions directly, I could have easily asked Miguel to pretend he was Shaggy during the meditation. Or I could have set it up so Miguel and Shaggy fought over the control box. Or I could have even brought the character of Miguel's friend Christo into the meditation. In this way Miguel and Christo could have argued over the box and Miguel could have imagined resolving a conflict with *Christo* with the help of Shaggy and Scooby.

If you are working with a teenager, consider explaining to him that imagining something in our minds helps us shift our way of thinking. Impress upon him that meditating will create change in his life. Encourage him to observe and experience the positive results that manifest in his life after meditation.

Although this meditation gives the child a tool for letting go of anger, feelings such as anger should not be ignored. They are important. In addition to a meditation about letting go, you can help your child discover the source of his anger and assist him to express it more effectively. For example, lead him through "The Happy Tree" meditation in Chapter 11 later in the week, but refer to the sad apples as angry apples. This meditation will help your child explore his anger and find out what his angry self needs.

UNDERSTANDING YOUR CHILD'S PERSPECTIVES AND LEARNING NEEDS

Most of us have forgotten what it's like to be a child. However, we can use meditation to remember. In meditation, we can look through the eyes of a child and see how he might experience what we plan to teach. This new perspective shows us the best course of action to take to introduce him to new concepts.

The following story shows how a parent uses this technique to come up with an effective and inspiring plan for teaching her child the concept of *surrender*.

> *It has been difficult for Olivia, Carmen's seven-year-old daughter, to "go with the flow." Olivia is easily upset when it's time to leave her house or give a toy back to a classmate. Carmen believes teaching her how to surrender will help Olivia through these transitions. When Carmen thinks about surrendering, she imagines a tall, gushing waterfall, and she considers guiding Olivia through a meditation about flowing water. However, Carmen realizes that Olivia's vision of surrender might be different from her own. Carmen opts to use meditation to better understand Olivia's world and find the best approach for her daughter to learn surrender.*

> *Carmen closes her eyes and takes three deep breaths. She allows her mind to let go of distracting thoughts, and then she states, "My intention for this meditation is to become a seven-year-old girl who experiences surrender in some way." Carmen trusts her meditation process and invites her inner senses to help her, and she soon begins to experience herself as a child. Within her meditation, Carmen becomes a seven-year-old girl awake in her bed at night. She notices she is afraid because it is dark in her bedroom, and her fear of the dark translates into wanting to stay awake. She looks on top of her dresser and sees a princess fairy*

doll. The fairy doll looks over at her as though she knows every thought the little girl is thinking. Carmen surrenders her fear of the dark to the princess fairy. She asks the doll to watch over her while she goes to sleep.

During Carmen's meditation, a young girl was afraid of the dark. Carmen now understands that the best way to introduce Olivia to the concept of letting go is to first ask her what she is afraid of. Olivia confides in her mother that she is afraid of forgetting her homework at school. Carmen asks, "Is there anyone or anything in your life, including yourself, that you trust to help you feel less afraid?" Olivia shares that she trusts her cat Sam with the things she is afraid of, and so Carmen leads her daughter through a meditation during which Olivia asks Sam to help her not be afraid.

Even though it was Olivia's challenge with transitions that originally prompted Carmen to teach her daughter about surrender, in her own meditation exercise Carmen saw a child experience surrender in a completely different situation. This is the purpose of the exercise. When we allow our inner senses to assist us, we often find a more appropriate and effective angle to take. Teaching Olivia how to let go of her fear about forgetting her homework helped her let go of her resistance to change.

The following meditation exercise follows the process Carmen used. It will help you to be a better meditation guide, as it gives you the background you need to lead your child through meditations.

Exercise 7

Experiencing a Child's World

1. Choose a topic you wish to teach your child; for example, gratitude. Close your eyes, take three calming breaths, and imagine yourself as a child. You do not need to imagine you are *your child*, nor do you need to imagine

you are *you* when you were a child. You simply need to imagine you are a child of the same age and possibly gender as the child you will be guiding and teaching.

2. Visualize yourself thinking and doing what this child would think and do. See what this child sees, hear what this child hears, and feel what this child feels. Allow yourself to follow this child's movements until you encounter a situation involving your topic. For example, if you chose gratitude, you might see a beautifully wrapped gift placed in front of you. Then notice how you handle the situation. See what this child sees, hear what this child hears, notice what this child thinks and feels.

   When you feel you have fully explored this child's experience of the concept, bring yourself out of the meditation. Immediately after your meditation, write down your experience and make notes about how you believe you can best teach this subject to your child, based on your meditation experience.

3. Now introduce the concept to your child. First ask questions, lots of questions. Questions are one of the best tools you have to inspire your child. Guide him into the mystery your lesson solves, piquing his interest. When a child is curious, teaching becomes effortless and learning becomes fun. For example, when teaching the concept of surrender, as in the previous example, you might ask, "What do you do when you get scared? What helps you feel better when you are afraid?" Now you have turned on your child's curiosity, and he is interested in following you through a journey to discover a new way to feel better when he is afraid.

4. Guide your child through a meditation you've created based on your meditation and your child's input. For example in Carmen's case, she realized that addressing her daughter's fears and whom she trusts with her fears was the best way to help her daughter understand surrender. After speaking with her, Carmen learned that Olivia was afraid of forgetting her homework and trusted her cat Sam. With this information, Carmen might have guided Olivia to imagine she is going to bed on a school night. Olivia imagines sitting with Sam before she gets into bed. She tells Sam how important her homework is, and asks him to please help her remember to bring it home with her the next day. Olivia takes a moment to experience how good it feels to let go of her worry. She feels warmth in her body, hears her favorite song, and sees stars sparkle all around her.

I work with children to help them overcome fears, improve their relationships, and process their emotions. Some of the meditations in this book were created for specific children in my practice, to help them with their particular challenges. Despite the collection of meditations I've produced over the years, I continue to create new ones inspired by my clients' unique challenges. With the two meditation creation methods in this chapter, you can help your child thrive physically, mentally, emotionally, and spiritually. When you use these methods in concert with your understanding of the ten senses, the learning styles, and other tips shared in this book, you will witness your child opening up in ways you never conceived, and living his life in harmony with himself and his world.

Remember, we are not teaching children to meditate, we are teaching meditation to children: offering them tools for exploration that will be useful when they choose to use them. So be creative and make your child's inner and outer explorations fun and exciting.

Above all, enjoy the journey you are taking with him. You will learn much about both of you along the way.

NOTES

CHAPTER 1

1. R.L. Wing. *The Tao of Power: A New Translation of the Tao Te Ching.* New York: Doubleday, 1986.

2. Ranganathan VK, Siemionow V, Liu JZ, Sahgal V, Yue GH. *From mental power to muscle power--gaining strength by using the mind.* Neuropsychologia. 2004;42(7):944-56.

3. *Personality and Individual Differences* 12 (1991): 1105–1116.; *Perceptual and Motor Skills* 62 (1986): 731–738.; *College Student Journal* 15 (1981): 140–146.; *The Journal of Creative Behavior* 19 (1985): 270–275.; *Journal of Clinical Psychology* 42 (1986): 161–164.; *Gedrag: Tijdschrift voor Psychologie* [Behavior: Journal of Psychology] 3 (1975): 167–182.

4. *Education* 107 (1986): 49–54.; *Education* 109 (1989): 302–304.; *Modern Science and Vedic Science* 1 (1987): 433–468.

5. Amy Adams. "Forget the latest toys—All kids really need is love." *Stanford Report*, July 12, 2006. http://news-service.stanford. edu/news/2006/july12/med-forget-071206.html

6. R. J. Davidson, J. Kabat-Zinn, J. Schumacher, M. Rosenkrantz, D. Muller, S. F. Santorelli, et al. (2003). "Alterations in brain and immune function produced by mindfulness meditation." *Psychosomatic Medicine, 65,* 564-570.

7. Shaila Dewan. "Emory's Little Tibet." *New York Times*, November 4, 2007

8. Leo F. Buscaglia. *Love: What Life Is All About.* Ballantine Books, 1996.

CHAPTER 2

1. *The Encyclopedia American International Edition*, 2001, Grolier Incorporated. Danbury, Connecticut. Volume 24, page 559.

2. *The Encyclopedia American International Edition*, 2001, Grolier Incorporated. Danbury, Connecticut. Volume 14, page 797.

CHAPTER 4

1. Zylowska L, Ackerman DL, Yang MH, Futrell JL, Horton NL, Hale TS, Pataki C, Smalley. Mindfulness meditation training in adults and adolescents with ADHD: a feasibility study. University of California- Los Angeles. *Journal of Attention Disorders.* 2008.

2. Linden, W. Practicing of meditation by school children and their levels of field dependence-independence, test anxiety, and reading achievement. *Journal of Consulting and Clinical Psychology.* 1973.

CHAPTER 5

1. Lipton, Bruce. *The Biology of Belief: Unleashing the Power of Consciousness, Matter & Miracles.* Santa Rosa, Calif.: Elite Books, 2005.

2. Kahlil Gibran. The Prophet. Alfred A. Knopf: New York 1923.

CHAPTER 6

1. Lucy Jo Palladino. *Dreamers, Discoverers and Dynamos.* New York: Ballantine Books, 1999.

CHAPTER 8

1. Children's Understanding of the Stream of Consciousness Study. *Stanford University. Society for Research in Child Development*, 1993.

2. Lipton, Bruce. *The Biology of Belief: Unleashing the Power of Consciousness, Matter & Miracles.* Santa Rosa, Calif.: Elite Books, 2005.

3. A.M. Krasner. *The Wizard Within: The Krasner Method of Clinical Hypnotherapy.* Irvine, Calif.: The American Board of Hypnotherapy Press, 1991. pp56-57.

CHAPTER 9

1. Rosalyn Bruyere. Wheels of Light: Chakras, Auras, and the Healing Energy of the Body. Fireside, 1994.

CHAPTER 11

1. Weiss, Brian L. *Many Lives, Many Masters: The True Story of a Prominent Psychiatrist, His Young Patient, and the Past-Life Therapy That Changed Both Their Lives.* New York: Simon & Schuster, 1988.

2. Carol Bowman. *Children's Past Lives: How Past Life Memories Affect your Child.* Bantam Books, 1998.

BIBLIOGRAPHY

Aldort, Naomi. *Raising Our Children, Raising Ourselves: Transforming Parent-Child Relationships from Reaction and Struggle to Freedom, Power and Joy.* Bothell, Washington: Book Publishers Network, 2006.

Bruyere, Rosalyn L. *Wheels of Light: Chakras, Auras, and the Healing Energy of the Body.* New York: Fireside, 1994.

Chopra, Deepak. *Quantum Healing: Exploring the Frontiers of Mind/Body Medicine.* New York: Bantam New Age Books, 1990.

Davis, Bruce. *The Magical Child Within You.* Berkeley, Calif.: Celestial Arts, 1985.

Ferrucci, Piero. *What Our Children Teach Us: Lessons in Joy, Love and Awareness.* New York: Warner Books, 2001.

Gawain, Shakti. *Meditations: Creative Visualization and Meditation Exercises to Enrich Your Life.* San Rafael, Calif.: New World Library, 1991.

Hart, Tobin. *The Secret Spiritual World of Children.* Maui: Inner Ocean Publishing, 2003.

Kohn, Alfie. *Unconditional Parenting: Moving from Rewards and Punishments to Love and Reason.* New York: Atria Books, 2005.

Krasner, A.M. *The Wizard Within: The Krasner Method of Clinical Hypnotherapy.* Irvine, Calif.: The American Board of

Hypnotherapy Press, 1991.

Lipton, Bruce. *The Biology of Belief: Unleashing the Power of Consciousness, Matter & Miracles.* Santa Rosa, Calif.: Elite Books, 2005.

Naparstek, Belleruth. *Invisible Heroes: Survivors of Trauma and How They Heal.* New York: Bantam Dell, 2004.

Palladino, Lucy Jo. *Dreamers, Discoverers & Dynamos: How to Help the Child Who Is Bright, Bored, and Having Problems in School.* New York: Ballantine, 1999.

Schunk, Dale H. *Learning Theories: An Educational Perspective.* Upper Saddle River, NJ: Pearson Education, 2004.

Weiss, Brian L. *Many Lives, Many Masters: The True Story of a Prominent Psychiatrist, His Young Patient, and the Past-Life Therapy That Changed Both Their Lives.* New York: Simon & Schuster, 1988.

INDEX

Z

Zen meditation, 87

About the Author

Sarah Wood Vallely is a parent-to-parent educator. She began working with children when she was ten years old in a classroom she set up in her home. Using a chalk board her father installed, she taught the neighborhood children everything from math to vocabulary. Sarah began working professionally with children in 1991. A former art teacher, Sarah now teaches meditation to children, helping children cope with depression, anxiety, stress and symptoms associated with ADHD.

When Sarah began teaching meditation to children in Los Angeles, her classes became a phenomenon. People without children came to see how someone could possibly persuade and inspire children to meditate. To help others learn what she does so effectively, Sarah also trains adults how to teach meditation to children in classrooms, at home, and in therapeutic settings. Sarah's program attracts students from across the U.S., Canada, Australia and Europe.

Sarah is first and foremost an artist. Using words and paint as her medium. The painting on the cover is a Picasso-inspired piece by Sarah depicting herself with her daughter. Sarah redides in Asheville, North Carolina.

Sarah has a bachelor's degree in Fine Art and her cross-cultural meditation training includes American Board of Hypnotherapy Certification, Vipassana (Buddhist), a four-year internship with a regression therapy master (Western Shamanism), Huna practitioner training (Hawaiian), Reiki, Level II (Japanese) and ongoing Yoga instruction (Hindu).

Become a certified meditation teacher for children...
To find out more about Sarah's globally recognized *Child Meditation Facilitators Training*, please go to: www.sarahwood.com

Additional articles, videos, books and other resources are also found at www.sarahwood.com

Another book by Sarah Wood Vallely ...
The Magic Gum Tree - A Children's Fantasy Story about Meditation (available on Amazon)

Honey, Felix and Timber, three possums from Australia, accidentally gain the power to travel through time. The curious possums quickly realize they are on a journey to become wizards. The characters travel to ancient India, explore mythical kingdoms, and earn their first wands. Young readers are swooped up in a thrilling adventure. At the same time, they learn ageless wisdom and valuable meditation practices. Techniques include breathing, mindfulness, and chakra balancing.